4/00

AIDS

An All-About Guide
for Young Adults

Alvin and Virginia Silverstein
and Laura Silverstein Nunn

Enslow Publishers, Inc.

44 Fadem Road	PO Box 38
Box 699	Aldershot
Springfield, NJ 07081	Hants GU12 6BP
USA	UK

http://www.enslow.com

Library of Congress Cataloging-in-Publication Data

Silverstein, Alvin.
    AIDS: an all-about guide for young adults / Alvin and Virginia Silverstein,
and Laura Silverstein Nunn.
        p. cm. — (Issues in focus)
    Includes bibliographical references and index.
    Summary: An overview of the history, biology, symptoms,
diagnosis, treatment, prevention, and future research of AIDS.
    ISBN 0-89490-716-6
    1. AIDS (Disease)—Juvenile literature. [1. AIDS (Disease)
2. Diseases.] I. Silverstein, Virginia B. II. Nunn, Laura Silverstein.
III. Title. IV. Series: Issues in focus (Hillside, N.J.)
RC607.A26S558   1999
616.97'92—dc21   98-37988
                                                         CIP
                                                         AC

Printed in the United States of America

10 9 8 7 6 5 4 3 2 1

To Our Readers:
All Internet addresses in this book were active and appropriate when we went
to press. Any comments or suggestions can be sent by e-mail to Comments@
enslow.com or to the address on the back cover.

Illustration Credits: AP Photo/Tim Shaffer, p. 82; Armando Waak, Pan
American Health Organization/UNAIDS, p. 42; Carlo Buscemi, p. 72;
Centers for Disease Control and Prevention (CDC), pp. 14, 25, 51, 110;
CDC HIV/AIDS Surveillance Report, p. 28; Corbis-Digital Stock, p. 76;
FDA Consumer, pp. 55, 59; Jonathan W. M. Gold, M.D., Cornell
University Medical College, New York, p. 12; Ken Kobre, USA/UNAIDS,
p. 92; © 1999 NAMES Project AIDS Memorial Quilt, Photo by Mark
Theissen, p. 119; National Institute of Allergy and Infectious Diseases, p.
80; Neal Preston/Corbis, p. 8; NIAID, NIH, p. 48; Owen Franken/Corbis,
p. 103; Public Health Service, p. 18; Public Health Service/CDC, pp.
39, 69; © 1996 by Randy Glasbergen, p. 75; R. Feldman, DCRT, NIH,
p. 32; Robert Reichert/Rockefeller University, p. 62; UNAIDS/Simon
Mathey, India, p. 30; UPI/Corbis-Bettmann, pp. 87, 97.

Cover Photo: © TSM/Charles Gupton.
The cover photo shows HIV specimen tubes.

Contents

Acknowledgments

The authors thank Dr. Larry Farrell, professor of Microbiology at Idaho State University, and Dr. Joe Margolick, M.D., Ph.D., of Johns Hopkins University, for their careful reading of the manuscript and their many helpful comments and suggestions.

A New Plague

On November 7, 1991, Earvin "Magic" Johnson, the superstar of basketball's Los Angeles Lakers, made an announcement that shocked the world: He was going to retire from professional basketball because he was infected with human immunodeficiency virus (HIV), the virus that causes AIDS. Johnson had found out about his condition accidentally: His application for a life insurance policy was rejected after routine medical tests were positive for HIV. Johnson spoke out frankly, stating that he had become infected by having sexual intercourse with too many women without using condoms. Although he still felt fine, he was retiring on the advice of the Lakers' team physician, Dr. Michael

5

Mellman. The doctor had informed Johnson that HIV damages the body's immune system, and the strenuous play of professional basketball could weaken him further, speeding up the progress of the illness. Johnson would devote himself to educating young people about AIDS and how to prevent it, spreading the word that "safe sex is the way to go."[1]

The reaction of Kevin McHale, a player for the Boston Celtics, was typical: "When you look at a big, healthy guy like Magic Johnson, you think this illness wouldn't attack someone like him. But it did."[2] If AIDS could strike someone like Johnson, then almost anyone might be at risk. Not everyone got the message, however. At the time, many Americans thought of AIDS as a disease largely confined to certain limited population groups, such as gay males and users of injected drugs—especially inner-city minorities. Rumors spread that Johnson must really have been bisexual, and most people expected that Johnson's announcement would soon be followed by news of serious illness and then his death.

As time passed, Magic Johnson's life brought a far different message to the world. Instead of quickly wasting away, the HIV-infected celebrity thrived. He soon found he could not stay away from pro basketball, and on September 29, 1992, Johnson ended his retirement and returned to the National Basketball Association. However, he quickly became a center of controversy when several players in the NBA expressed concerns about their own health with Johnson in the game. Johnson was forced to retire again, despite efforts by Dr. Mellman to convince the players that there was practically no chance of contracting the virus from Johnson during a game of basketball. Johnson was saddened by the fact that a lack of AIDS education had kept him from being accepted by his fellow athletes. His experiences were similar to those of thousands of other people with HIV/AIDS: He had to quit a job he loved, was the subject of embarrassing speculations about his sex life, and was regarded with fear by many of his coworkers.[3]

Magic Johnson did not give up on his dream to play in the NBA again. In January 1996, he once again came out of retirement. His health was good, and he felt strong and was eager to play. This time, no one seemed to have a problem with Johnson's decision. Since his diagnosis in 1991, a greater understanding and acceptance of HIV and AIDS had developed. As Reggie Miller, a player for the Indiana Pacers, commented excitedly, "If he does hear any objections, they haven't had their HIV education."[4]

Johnson's triumphant return to pro basketball also reflected some important changes in the realities of AIDS. When his HIV infection was first diagnosed, it seemed to be a true death sentence. Only one drug—zidovudine, or AZT—had been approved for treating AIDS, and its effectiveness was limited. In the years that followed, however, new drugs were developed and approved, and doctors began to use them in combinations that worked far better. Magic Johnson was started on AZT therapy right after his diagnosis, and two more drugs were later added. By mid-1998, his immune system was still strong, and the amount of HIV in his blood was too small to be detected.[5] After he retired from basketball at the end of the 1996 season, he actively pursued business interests (including a part-ownership of the Lakers, a T-shirt company, and a new movie theater complex), made appearances for his nonprofit AIDS foundation, briefly hosted a late-night television talk show, and enjoyed family life with his wife and children. His attitude has remained positive. "I've always enjoyed challenges," he says. "I never, ever accept losing. That's why I think I'm doing well."[6]

Celebrities like Magic Johnson have made a great contribution toward spreading information about AIDS, a disease that no one had even heard of before 1981. The disease, too, has been spreading explosively during the past two

••••••••••••• *Magic Johnson speaks out to young people about the dangers of HIV.*

decades. Appearing at first in very small numbers among a few specific groups in a few small areas, AIDS has now become a truly worldwide problem. According to data reported by the Joint United Nations Programme on HIV/AIDS in 1998, an estimated 30.6 million people are infected with HIV, the virus that causes AIDS, and about 11.7 million have died from AIDS since the epidemic began—2.3 million in 1997 alone. If current trends continue, warns the Global AIDS Policy Coalition, as many as 70 million people will have been infected by HIV by the end of the year 2000.[7]

In the United States and other industrially developed nations, worldwide trends, fortunately, are not continuing. In 1996, for the first time since the AIDS epidemic began, the annual number of deaths from this disease in the United States decreased by 28 percent (from 48,371 in 1995 to

34,947 in 1996); the number of new cases of AIDS also decreased. The trend continued in 1997, with only 14,339 deaths—a drop of nearly 60 percent—and 31,153 new cases diagnosed.[8] This encouraging news reflects the enormous progress that medical science has made on the AIDS front: In less than two decades, researchers have discovered the cause of the disease (the human immunodefiency virus) and much about how it damages the body. They have developed tests for HIV infection, ways to stop its spread, and effective treatments. For the first time, some medical specialists have voiced the hope that AIDS may no longer be an automatic death sentence but rather a long-term, chronic condition that can be managed while the person still lives a fairly normal life. There have even been cautious speculations that AIDS can ultimately be cured.

However, "the good news does not mean that AIDS is over and if we act like it is, it never will be," says Daniel Zingale, executive director of AIDS Action Council in Washington, D.C.[9] Despite the medical advances, AIDS treatments are still far too costly to be used in much of the world, and they do not work for everyone. It is still much easier to prevent AIDS than to cure it. Education is helping to change the attitudes and practices that have contributed to the spread of our newest plague, but there are still many mistaken ideas about AIDS. Some of the people most at risk do not seem to recognize the danger or, if they do know better, do not always act wisely. Although AIDS can affect people of all ages, all races, and both sexes, teenagers and young adults are the prime targets for HIV infection.[10] "One in four people with HIV was infected before age 21," noted Donna Futterman, director of the Adolescent AIDS Program at Montefiore Medical Center in Bronx, New York.[11] Young people have the greatest need for solid information to make decisions that can affect the length and quality of their lives.

2

The History of AIDS

In the fall of 1980, immunologist Michael Gottlieb had just started his new job as an assistant professor at UCLA. Looking for ideas for a research project, he asked the medical residents he supervised to keep an eye out for any patients with interesting problems involving the immune system, which defends the body against disease. In November, one of the residents told Dr. Gottlieb about a young man with a yeast infection in his throat. It was so severe that the patient could hardly breathe. This kind of infection usually occurs only in people with defects in their immune defenses. But this patient was an otherwise healthy young man. Two days later the patient came down with

10

an unusual kind of pneumonia, caused by a microscopic parasite called *Pneumocystis carinii*. There was something peculiar about his blood tests, too. One particular type of white blood cells, called CD4 cells, or helper T cells, was missing. Gottlieb wondered what could have knocked out a whole set of immune cells, but he could not find any clues in the medical literature.

The patient's medical records revealed that he had previously suffered from a number of sexually transmitted diseases, and in a conversation he mentioned that he was gay. That particular detail did not seem important at first. But then, in January 1981, a Los Angeles doctor, Joel Weisman, sent Gottlieb a patient who was suffering from severe immune-system problems. He had been running a fever for three months, suffered from persistent diarrhea, and had fungus infections growing on his fingernails, a yeast infection in his mouth, and severe skin rashes. He had had a number of herpes infections and had lost thirty pounds. His lymph nodes (masses of germ-fighting tissue) were swollen, his white cell count was very low, and he was having trouble breathing. Tests showed that he, too, had Pneumocystis carinii pneumonia (PCP), and he, too, was gay. Dr. Weisman told Gottlieb that he had one more patient with similar symptoms, and he was also gay. In April still another gay patient showed the same kind of symptoms. Something unusual seemed to be happening in the local gay community. Alarmed, Gottlieb called a doctor at the Los Angeles County Department of Public Health and discovered that another gay male had died unusually. This patient had had pneumonia caused by cytomegalovirus, a herpesvirus that does not normally kill.[1]

Meanwhile, specialists in New York had noticed a curious cluster of cases of Kaposi's sarcoma that had recently appeared in the gay male community there. Kaposi's sarcoma (KS) is a rather rare kind of cancer in

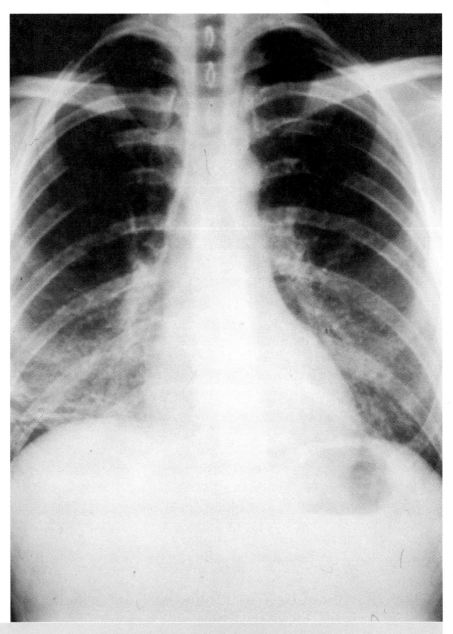

Chest X ray showing pneumocystis pneumonia.

which painless purplish spots that look like birthmarks or bruises appear on the skin. In the developed countries it occurs only in a few elderly men of Mediterranean ancestry. In these men KS is a very mild, slow-growing cancer, and the patients usually die years later of something else. A more severe and rapid-developing form of KS is found in some areas of Africa, however, and the young gay males seemed to have this more serious type.

Michael Gottlieb's friend at the Department of Public Health, Dr. Wayne Shandera, suggested sending their report on PCP to the Centers for Disease Control (CDC) in Atlanta for publication in their weekly newsletter, *Morbidity and Mortality Weekly Report (MMWR)*. This was a way to get the news out to people in the medical community quickly. Their report was published in the June 5, 1981, issue of *MMWR*.[2]

Detective Story

In the days that followed, more reports about strange combinations of illnesses in gay men flooded in. The CDC formed a special task force to investigate the outbreak of previously rare diseases. Within a few months, they had more than one hundred cases to study. Some had Kaposi's sarcoma, some had PCP, and some had both. In addition, some patients suffered from a variety of strange infections. Some had fungus growths in the mouth and throat that made eating and speaking difficult. Some had herpes infections with open sores in the mouth or on the genitals that did not heal for months. There were also fungus and protozoan infections that are usually found in animals, and a serious bacterial infection that cave explorers sometimes catch from bat excrement. What these varied infections had in common was that they were all opportunistic—they rarely occurred except in people whose immune systems were damaged. All the victims were gay, and most lived in just three places: New York City, San Francisco, and Los Angeles. They had typically been sexually promiscuous, averaging more than a thousand sexual partners each. Most of the men had been treated with antibiotics for sexually transmitted diseases such as syphilis, gonorrhea, and herpes. They had suffered from hepatitis infections and diarrhea-causing parasitic infections. Many were also heavy users of recreational drugs—particularly forms of nitrites called poppers, which are inhaled to increase the pleasurable feelings of sexual activity.[3]

The CDC task force, headed by Dr. James Curran, searched through their disease records and found no cases of the "gay plague" occurring before 1979, so this was apparently a new disease. But what was causing it? Researchers speculated that the use of poppers was the key:

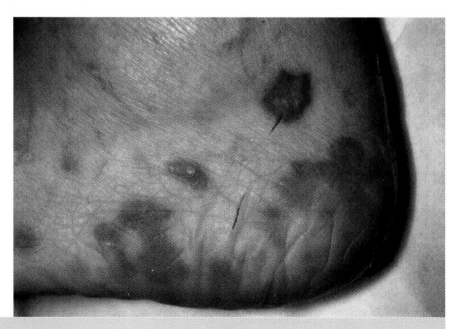

Kaposi's sarcoma, a rare type of cancer, is sometimes seen in patients who have AIDS.

Perhaps there had been a contaminated lot of them. An immune-suppressing effect in the nitrites, which had been observed in laboratory animals, might also be the cause. Other researchers suggested that the repeated infections with sexually transmitted diseases these men had suffered had produced a sort of "immune overload." Another popular theory held that oral and anal sex, commonly practiced by gay men, could introduce semen into the body and provoke an immune reaction against the foreign chemicals it contained. Still another possibility was some sort of sexually transmitted germ. The CDC researchers painstakingly interviewed patients (or relatives, friends, and lovers if the patients had died) and compared their answers with those of a matched group of young men who were not sick. The disease appeared to be sexually transmitted. In fact, the task force discovered clusters of cases among men who had sex partners in common; one such group was in Los Angeles. One patient in New York was found to have been a sex partner of four of the men in Los Angeles, as well as of four patients in New York.[4]

Medical researchers began to refer to the new disease as GRID (gay-related immune deficiency), and the popular press played up the sensational aspects of this apparently sex-related health problem. Some religious leaders claimed that the gay plague was God's punishment of homosexuals for their lifestyle. Soon, however, it became obvious that the new public health threat was much broader. The same kinds of opportunistic infections resulting from damage to the immune system began to appear among other groups. The first new group to be hit hard by the disease consisted of drug addicts who used injected drugs (including homosexual men, heterosexual men, and women) and their sex partners. Cases also began to appear among people who had received blood transfusions or treatments with blood products, as well as in recent immigrants from Haiti. The illness transmitted by blood did not play favorites—it affected people of both sexes and all ages, from infants to the elderly. Reports also began to come in from other parts of the United States and other countries of the world. The name AIDS (*a*cquired *i*mmune *d*eficiency *s*yndrome) was adopted. *Acquired* was used to distinguish the condition from inherited defects of the immune system that are present at birth. *Syndrome* refers to a collection of symptoms and signs of illness that commonly occur together. Doctors were still not certain this was a single *disease*, but it seemed increasingly evident that some kind of infection was involved. The blood-clotting factors used to treat people with hemophilia ("bleeders disease") were filtered to remove bacteria and fungi but could still transmit AIDS, so the cause of the disease had to be a microorganism small enough to pass through the filters—a virus. Researchers began an active hunt for the AIDS virus.

Who Discovered the AIDS Virus?

Who really discovered the AIDS virus? For years this question was the center of a heated debate. Two research teams, one in the United States and one in France, had good claims. The prizes at stake were great: not only fame and glory—perhaps even a Nobel Prize—for making a great medical discovery, but also money for their research institute from patent rights for tests, vaccines, and treatments based on the discovery.

The American team was headed by Dr. Robert Gallo, director of the Laboratory of Tumor Cell Biology at the National Cancer Institute in Bethesda, Maryland. In 1980 Gallo had discovered the first human cancer virus, HTLV-I (human T-cell leukemia virus, type I). This virus infects the type of white blood cells called T cells and causes them to multiply uncontrollably. HTLV-I is what scientists call a

Patient Zero

In his dramatic book about the early years of the AIDS epidemic, *And the Band Played On*, journalist Randy Shilts identified a French-Canadian flight attendant, Gaetan Dugas, as Patient Zero. Attractive and charming, Dugas was implicated—either personally or through his sexual contacts—in at least 40 of the first 248 AIDS cases reported in the United States. In 1981, Dugas told doctors trying to trace the origin of the disease that during the previous ten years he had had at least 2,500 sexual encounters, mainly with men he met in gay bars and bathhouses in California and New York. Patient Zero never fully understood his role in spreading the deadly virus. He told a doctor, "It's my right to do what I want with my body," and he continued to be sexually active until the disease killed him in 1984.[5]

retrovirus. *Retro-* means "backwards" and retroviruses reverse the usual process by which cells translate the hereditary blueprints in the genes into the biochemicals they need.

Normally a cell's hereditary information is recorded in a kind of code, in a chemical called deoxyribonucleic acid (DNA). Portions of the DNA, the genes, are used as patterns from which a simpler form of hereditary chemical, RNA, is made. The cell then uses the RNA pattern to make proteins, which form the cell's structures and conduct its chemical reaction. Retroviruses do not have any DNA, just RNA. These viruses hijack the cells they infect and use them for slave labor. Using a viral chemical called reverse transcriptase (RT), the cell makes a DNA copy of the virus's RNA, then starts mass-producing new virus materials. Positive tests for RT show that a retrovirus is present, because normal body cells do not produce this chemical.

Because there was evidence that some of the T cells of AIDS patients were being selectively destroyed, Dr. Gallo reasoned that the AIDS virus must target T cells, the way HTLV-I does, only it destroys the cells instead of causing them to multiply. Perhaps it was a variation of the HTLV family. Gallo's research team found retroviruses in tissue samples from several AIDS patients, including two gay men and a woman from Haiti. The team named the new virus HTLV-III and submitted research papers announcing its discovery to the journal *Science* for publication. They wanted to grow the patients' helper T cells in culture dishes so that they would have more virus material to work with, but the cultures all died. Gallo put the specimens away in a freezer to work on later, when better culture techniques were developed.

Meanwhile, researchers in France were also becoming convinced that a retrovirus was the cause of AIDS. They

theorized that there might be larger amounts of the virus in people at an earlier stage of the disease, before so many of their T cells had been killed off. Dr. Luc Montagnier, chief of viral oncology at the Pasteur

Dr. Robert Gallo conducted AIDS research at the National Cancer Institute's Laboratory of Tumor Cell Biology.

Institute in Paris, isolated a retrovirus from a patient with lymphadenopathy (swollen lymph nodes) and named it LAV (for lymphadenopathy-associated virus). He corresponded with Dr. Gallo, and the two laboratories exchanged tissue samples. Articles by Gallo, his associate Myron Essex, and Luc Montagnier were all published in the same issue of *Science* in May of 1983. Although the French group had not been able to grow the virus in culture either, they filed an application for a patent on a blood test based on their discovery.[6]

In May 1984, the Gallo group announced that they had found the virus in forty-eight patients, grown large amounts of it in culture, analyzed some chemicals on the surface of the virus and found them to be related to HTLV-I and II, and developed a technique for detecting antibodies that could be used as the basis for a test to screen donated blood for the virus. Margaret Heckler, the Secretary of the U.S. Department of Health and Human Services at the time, called a press conference to announce the achievement. "Today we add another miracle to the long honor roll of American medicine and science," she said proudly.[7]

The United States government filed for patents on the process of mass-producing the virus and on the antibody test, and the French were outraged. *They* had discovered the virus, they claimed, and applied for a patent on a test a full year before. Gallo stated that the French had not proved that the virus was the cause of AIDS and pointed to research notebooks from his laboratory dating from 1982 that showed results similar to those of the French. The French researchers argued that LAV, which was very similar to Gallo's virus samples, was not a leukemia virus but belonged to a different retrovirus family, and later studies supported this view. The battle raged on in the pages of scientific journals, in the popular press, and in the courts.

In 1986 an international committee recommended that

the AIDS virus should be named HIV (for *h*uman *i*mmunodeficiency *v*irus), and in 1987 United States president Ronald Reagan and French premier Jacques Chirac made a joint announcement that the legal dispute had been resolved. The U.S. Department of Health and Human Services and the Pasteur Institute of Paris would share the patent royalties and would donate 80 percent of them to a new international AIDS research foundation. Robert Gallo and Luc Montagnier worked together to prepare a history of the study of human retroviruses and the development of the AIDS antibody test, recognizing the contributions of both research teams.[8]

That was not the end of the story, however. A *Chicago Tribune* article in 1989 suggested that Gallo's group might have committed scientific fraud, and official investigations were launched. Charges of misconduct were made against Gallo's group, then later dropped.[9]

In an attempt to end the dispute once and for all, in July 1994 the U.S. National Institutes of Health (NIH) agreed to a revised patent agreement. It was more favorable to the Pasteur Institute of Paris. Dr. Harold Varmus, head of the NIH, also acknowledged officially that "scientists at NIH used a virus provided to them by Institut Pasteur to invent the American HIV test kit."[10] Dr. Luc Montagnier, whose Pasteur Institute had aggressively pushed the case since the *Chicago Tribune* article appeared, said he was glad the argument was over at last. "The sides might still not agree about what was done by Dr. Gallo," he told an interviewer. "Dr. Gallo did admit to me privately he made a mistake in not quoting in his paper that he used our virus. But we will set those things aside now."[11] AIDS activist Martin E. Delaney, executive director of Project Inform in San Francisco, expressed the public's feelings of relief. "It's not a productive use of anybody's time to keep squabbling over this," he remarked.[12]

Was AIDS Really a New Disease?

Although Patient Zero may have been the source of a mini-epidemic of AIDS cases, he was far from the first person with AIDS. Searching back through medical records, medical scientists found that there actually were numerous cases from the 1970s and earlier that fit the general profile of the disease. Examination of blood and tissue samples that had been saved from autopsies and medical studies revealed traces of the virus as far back as the 1960s.

In 1999, the AIDS virus that has infected about 30 million people worldwide was found to apparently come from a similar virus in a subspecies of chimpanzee in Africa. The virus was identified in the tissues of a wild-caught chimpanzee named Marilyn. The virus, SIVcpz (for *s*imian *i*mmunodeficiency *v*irus *chimp*anzee), does not cause illness in chimpanzees.[13]

A virus, like other parasites, needs living hosts to survive and spread. Viruses that kill all their hosts, or kill them before they have a chance to be transmitted to new hosts, will not be very successful in the fight for survival. But viruses in general and the immunodeficiency viruses in particular have an enormous ability to change from one virus generation to the next. (A virus generation may be counted in hours or even minutes.) Scientists have already discovered two different strains of HIV and a number of varieties (subtypes) within the strains. This great variation provides plenty of opportunities for the evolution of successful virus forms. Typically, when a disease germ jumps from one host species to another, it is at first more deadly in its new host. But gradually new forms, better able to live off the host without killing it too quickly, appear.

Researchers believe that today's HIV strains were transmitted to people in Africa, perhaps a century or so ago. We will probably never know exactly how the cross-species jump occurred, but it could have occurred through cuts or wounds acquired when hunters killed chimpanzees and monkeys for food. (Chimpanzees have also been observed killing and eating baboons, sooty mangabeys, and other kinds of monkeys.)[14]

Evolutionary biologist Paul Ewald suggests that after SIV somehow made the jump to humans in the African rain forests and started evolving into HIV, the new disease at first spread slowly, during occasional contacts between villages. Then dramatic cultural changes came into play. Civil wars and industrial development promoted migration from the rural areas into the cities. Many men went to the cities to find work, sending their earnings back to their families in the villages. Cut off from the tribal traditions, they were lonely and more likely to visit prostitutes and engage in other promiscuous sexual behavior. Sexually transmitted diseases spread rapidly along trade routes. Frequent infections with other diseases aggravated the problem, since cells of the immune system are most vulnerable to attack by HIV when they are actively stimulated to fight other invading microbes. The use and reuse of hypodermic needles to give injections of antibiotics and also for drug abuse provided another effective means of spreading the AIDS virus. Meanwhile, the development of air travel greatly increased the contacts of Africans with people from other continents. Frequent and promiscuous sexual contacts helped promote the development of more deadly strains of the virus.

Because there were so many opportunities for spreading the virus from one person to another, the virus could survive even if it killed its hosts fairly quickly. The freer sexual practices that had become common in the United States, especially among gays, provided an ideal "culture medium" for growing and spreading sexually transmitted microbes.

3

What Is AIDS?

At twenty-one, Dawn was fulfilling all her dreams. When she was seventeen, she had fooled around with injected drugs and had unprotected sex with the man she shared needles with, but since then she had turned her life around. She had gone to college, gotten married, worked at a job she liked, and had a beautiful baby girl, Lindsay. After three months of "normal babyhood—breast-feeding and sleepless nights and dirty diapers and learning to be a mommy," Dawn noticed that Lindsay would turn blue around the mouth when she cried. Her doctor said the baby had viral pneumonia. A month later, when Lindsay was not gaining weight and seemed slow in developing, the doctors asked Dawn if

23

she had ever done anything that could have put her at risk for AIDS. Blood tests soon showed that both she and Lindsay were HIV positive, although her husband tested negative. By the time Lindsay was a year old, she had developed AIDS, and she died at eighteen months. While coping with her baby's illness, and later, while grieving for her, Dawn often forgot to take her own medicine (drugs to prevent pneumonia), and several times she had bouts of pneumonia and had to be hospitalized. Her family was very supportive, though. Her parents came over to cook for her when she was too weak to care for herself, and her husband stuck by her, although, she says, "He closes right up if I get too emotional. . . . He cannot bear to see my pain."[1]

For Robert, a thirty-six-year-old X-ray technician in Queens, New York, AIDS means waking in the night to the sound of his lover retching, burning with fever and racked with pain. It means endless rounds of taking his partner to the doctor, feeling elated when the treatments are going well and fearful when the illness flares up again. It means keeping secrets—from his lovers family, from people at his job, and from some of their friends. It means filling out forms and coping with red tape for medical benefits and disability income. "I'm so tired all the time," Robert says, "I feel like I'm going to break down and get sick. But I can't. I'm all he has."[2]

Defining a Disease

AIDS is a collection of diseases caused by infections that may hit a person whose immune system has been weakened by HIV. Such opportunistic infections include PCP, various fungus and protozoan infections, and tuberculosis occurring in places other than the lungs. AIDS can also include some direct effects of HIV infection, such as a severe loss of weight and muscle tissue and damage to the brain and mental functions. Doctors detect HIV and follow the course of the disease by measuring the amount of the virus in the blood and tissues. They also count the number of a type of white blood cells called CD4 cells (the helper T cells) that are infected and destroyed by HIV.

It took a long time and a lot of research to arrive at this definition of AIDS. The 1987 definition of AIDS in adults and adolescents included laboratory evidence of HIV infection, various opportunistic infections and rare cancers, neurologic disease due to infection of the brain by HIV or by the parasite *Toxoplasma*, and the HIV wasting syndrome (a persistent drop in weight and loss of muscle tissue).[3]

During the years that followed, there were growing complaints about the 1987 definition. The main problem

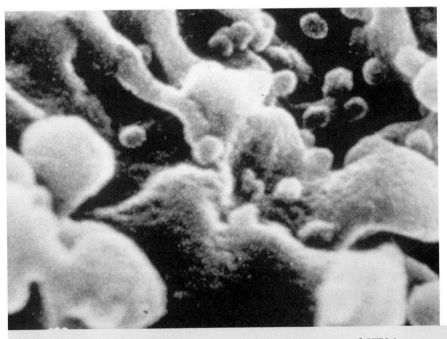

T-4 lymphocytes become infected with HIV. The amount of HIV in a patient's blood is monitored by his or her doctor.

was that the definition had been formed in observations of gay male patients, and some conditions found in women with AIDS were not included. As a result, many women with AIDS were ignored—both in the statistics and in the medical diagnosis that would qualify them to receive health and disability benefits. As a slogan of the activist group ACT UP put it, "Women don't get AIDS, they just die from it."[4] The CDC argued that keeping the definition constant kept the monitoring of the epidemic consistent; if they made a major change in the definition, there would be a huge apparent increase in the AIDS statistics. Eventually the CDC decided to expand the definition, partly to be able to catch cases earlier and permit patients to benefit from new preventive treatments that were being developed. The revised case definition, which went into effect at the beginning of 1993, added conditions such as invasive cervical cancer, recurrent pneumonia, and pulmonary tuberculosis, as well as a CD4 cell count below 200 cells per cubic millimeter of blood.[5] (The normal range for CD4 cells is from 500 to 1,500 cells per cubic millimeter.)

When the statistics for 1993 came in, the expected increase in the number of cases did indeed occur: There was a 111 percent increase in the number of new cases compared with 1992, and 54 percent were reported on the basis of conditions just added to the definition. The increases in new cases were greater among women than among men, among blacks and Hispanics than among whites, and among young people aged 13–19 years and 20–24 years in comparison with older age groups.[6]

AIDS Symptoms

The new case definition adopted by the CDC in 1993 also established a series of categories from the early to the late stages of HIV/AIDS disease. First, there may be a short,

If You Are HIV Positive, Do You Have AIDS?

Many people are confused about the difference between HIV infection and AIDS. Infection with the virus can lead to the disease, but AIDS does not develop immediately. It takes time for HIV to multiply and damage the immune system—sometimes ten years or longer after the original infection. During this time there may be no symptoms. The person is infected—and can pass on the infection to others—but is not actually sick.

Health authorities consider that a person has AIDS when there is evidence of HIV infection (a positive laboratory test) and the person develops certain illnesses, such as opportunistic infections, rare cancers such as Kaposi's sarcoma or lymphoma of the brain, or HIV wasting syndrome. A severe drop in the number of CD4 cells, either to less than 200 per microliter (cubic millimeter) of blood or less than 14 percent of the total number of lymphocytes, is also a sign of AIDS.

flulike illness following the first exposure to HIV. Then, there is a long period in which the person is infected but does not show any symptoms. This period can last for years, and the person may be unaware that he or she is infected. In the next stage, the lymph nodes become swollen, because the body is battling the multiplying virus. Finally, a variety of symptoms and complications appear. Loss of appetite, weight loss, fever, rashes, night sweats, and fatigue are typical symptoms of AIDS. The person may also develop memory loss, confusion, and various other mental problems due to infection of the brain by the virus. Weakening of the immune system opens the way for opportunistic infections such as Pneumocystis carinii pneumonia (PCP),

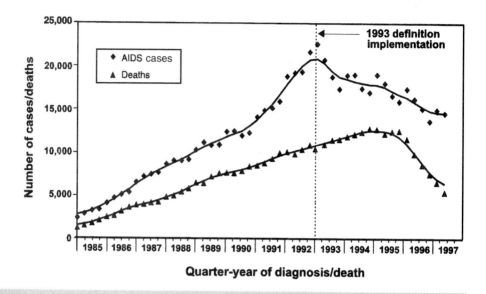

Estimated numbers of AIDS cases and deaths in the United States, from January 1985 to June 1997. After a change in the definition of AIDS in 1993, a corresponding increase in cases occurred.

Mycobacterium avium complex (MAC), toxoplasmosis, cytomegalovirus (CMV) and herpes infections, and CMV retinitis (which can cause blindness). The breakdown of the body's defenses against disease may also allow various cancers to develop, including Kaposi's sarcoma (KS), lymphomas, and invasive cervical cancer. Another common effect is the HIV wasting syndrome, a severe loss of weight and muscle tissue.[7]

Ironically, most of the symptoms typically linked with AIDS are caused not by the infection itself but by the other diseases that set in after HIV has dangerously weakened the body's defenses. Coughing and shortness of breath are symptoms of pneumonia. Rashes and sores on the skin or in the mouth may be caused by fungus or herpesvirus infections. Confusion, memory loss, and other mental problems may be due to HIV infection, but they can also be caused by attack on the brain by the parasite *Toxoplasma*. The purplish spots on the skin of some people with AIDS are signs of Kaposi's sarcoma. The great variety of opportunistic microbes that can attack a person with AIDS is responsible for the great variety of symptoms, which made it difficult at first for medical researchers to determine that they were dealing with a single disease. (If AIDS had been named later, it probably would not have been called a syndrome, but rather HIV disease.)

The first symptoms of AIDS—the chills and fever of a brief flulike illness—may not occur, or they may not be recognized as linked to an HIV infection. Actually, they are largely due not to the effects of the virus itself, but to the body's efforts to fight it—as is the case for other viral infections, as well.

Who Gets AIDS?

When AIDS first appeared in the United States, it seemed to be a disease of gay men. Since then, however, it has become evident that it can strike people of both sexes, all ages, all races, and all sexual orientations. In the United States, the largest group of people with AIDS is still men who have sex with men (48 percent of all cases reported up to the end of 1997), but injection drug users account for 25 percent (plus an additional 6 percent who fall into both exposure groups). The proportions of both men and women who acquired AIDS through heterosexual contact, after increasing steadily for years, dropped somewhat in 1997, to 9 percent of the total up to that point. Children under thirteen years of age accounted for only 8,086 (a little more than one percent) of the total of 641,086 cases reported in the United States through the end of 1997.[8] The majority of AIDS cases (482,168, or 75 percent) had been diagnosed in people from age twenty-five to forty-four. Blacks and Hispanics were represented far in excess of their proportions in the general population (230,029 and 115,354 cases, or 36 percent and 18 percent of the cases, respectively).[9] While AIDS was no longer the leading killer of all adults in the twenty-five to forty-four age group after the decreases in AIDS deaths in 1996, it was still the leading killer in that age group for black men and women.[10]

Worldwide, the AIDS picture looks quite different. According to United Nations estimates, as of the end of 1997, more than 30 million people were living with HIV infection. About 40 percent of them were women, and nearly 4 percent were children. An additional 14,400 adults and 1,600 children were being infected each day. Africa has been the continent hit hardest by AIDS: At the end of 1997,

Students at a boys' school in India receive information about HIV and AIDS in an AIDS awareness class.

an estimated 21 million Africans were infected with HIV, and an additional 10 million had died of AIDS (83 percent of all the AIDS deaths in the world). In some parts of Africa, one in four adults were infected with the virus. Infection rates have been growing rapidly in Asia, where no serious epidemics occurred until the late 1980s. More than 6 million Asians were living with HIV infection as of the end of 1997. In Cambodia, 10 percent of blood donors in 1995 were found to be infected, compared with 0.1 percent in 1991. Studies in 1997 found that 1 in 30 pregnant women, 1 in 16 soldiers and policemen, and close to 1 in 2 prostitutes tested positive for HIV infection in that country. In Myanmar the infection rate among prostitutes went from 4 percent in 1992 to 20 percent in 1996, and nearly two thirds of injection drug users were infected. Another sad statistic: More than 8 million children worldwide under age fifteen have lost their mothers or both parents to HIV and AIDS. Among the few bright spots in both HIV infection rates and AIDS diagnoses were drops in Thailand and Uganda, where community groups are helping to reduce unsafe sex and drug use. The rates also dropped in São Paulo, Brazil, which has budgeted more funds for making the newer combination drug therapies available to patients.[11]

HIV: The AIDS Virus

It was lucky for the world that the AIDS epidemic appeared when it did and not twenty years earlier. In 1960, retroviruses had not even been imagined, and scientists had just begun to develop the powerful techniques of molecular biology that were brought to bear on the new medical threat. The massive research effort prompted by the war on cancer campaign in the 1970s helped lay the foundation for the fast progress in HIV research. In a brief time, scientists have now learned more about the human immunodeficiency virus

A computer-generated model of HIV shows the tiny knobs of protein that cover the virus's outer surface.

than about virtually any other disease-causing germ.

In electron micrographs, magnified about two hundred thousand times, the HIV virus (or virion) looks like a pincushion. It is a tiny sphere, about one ten-thousandth of a millimeter in diameter, studded with tiny knobs. Its outer shell has the same double-layered structure of lipid (a fatty substance) and protein as the outer membrane of a typical body cell. The knobs sticking out of the sphere are made up of a protein called gp120. Inside this outer "coat" is a core containing HIV's RNA.

The life cycle of HIV has two main parts. The first part starts when an HIV virion attaches itself to the outside of a cell. Its outer membrane merges with the cell's outer membrane, and the material from the virus's core moves into the cell. There it is like an uninvited guest that not only makes itself at home but soon starts running the household. Using the materials of the host cell, the viral enzymes go to work, copying the HIV genetic material. The completed DNA copy of the HIV genes will be copied every time the cell divides and reproduces its own genes. In some cells the life cycle may stop there. The HIV genes may remain quietly hidden among the host cell's genes, apparently doing nothing at all. This situation may go on for years. But then something may happen to start off the second part of the virus's life cycle—for example, when an infected white blood cell is activated to fight invading germs. At that point the hidden virus uses its host cell as a factory to produce and release new HIV virions.

The Body Defends Itself

The body's first line of defense against invading germs is a set of barriers: the skin that covers the outer surface and the slippery, mucus-covered membranes that line the mouth, nose, and other passages that lead into the body. A cut or sore in these coverings might allow germs to slip into the bloodstream. Some germs are also capable of infecting mucous membranes. Cold viruses, for example, can infect cells in the respiratory tract; HIV can infect cells in the lining of the rectum, vagina, and penis.

Cells that are attacked by a virus release various chemicals. Some of them act as distress signals that call in white blood cells, the body's roving defenders. Several kinds of white blood cells help fight invading germs. Some, called macrophages (literally, "big cells that eat"), gobble up invading germs, destroying them before they can infect cells. Others, the lymphocytes, are able to recognize foreign chemicals, such as the proteins on the outer coat of a virus. Some of these lymphocytes, called B cells, produce antibodies, proteins that fit parts of virus proteins. Antibodies attach to viruses, preventing them from attacking their target cells or making them easier for macrophages to destroy. Antibodies also tag virus-infected cells, marking them for destruction. Several kinds of lymphocytes are called T cells. Killer T cells kill infected cells and cancer cells. Helper T cells stimulate B cells to multiply and produce antibodies. The macrophages, T cells, and B cells are constantly communicating with one another and coordinating their activities by way of a stream of chemical messengers carried by the bloodstream and tissue fluids.

Once a person has antibodies that protect against a particular virus, some of the antibody-producing cells are kept "on file" in the body, ready to leap into action if the same type of virus attacks again. It generally takes about two weeks to make an adequate supply of antibodies to fight a virus the body has never met before; during that time the viruses multiply while the body's less specific defenses try to keep them in check.

When HIV Attacks

"If I were a devil creating a malicious virus to cause the most problems for the human race," says Dr. Luc Montagnier, "the virus would be [the] AIDS [virus]. The virus has found the Achilles heel of the immune system."[12] The main targets of HIV are the body's own defenders, particularly the helper T lymphocytes and the macrophages.

When HIV invades the body, a furious battle rages at first. Fever and other general defenses try to keep the virus in check. The cells of the immune system build up antibodies and targeted killer T cells to zero in on the foreign germ. Meanwhile, virus particles attach to a protein called CD4 on the surface of helper T cells and some other cells. Researchers have recently found that for an AIDS virus to fuse with the membrane of its target cell, it must also bind to another surface protein, or receptor. At least five receptors recognized by HIV have already been found; one that HIV can use especially effectively is called CCR5.

Once inside its target cell, HIV begins to reproduce, using the cell as a factory to mass-produce virus particles. In helper T cells, virus production is fast and furious, and the release of the new virions may kill the cell. The body steps up its production of T cells, trying to replace those that are lost. Meanwhile, HIV also reproduces in infected macrophages, though more slowly, and the virions can leave the host cell without killing it. Migrating macrophages may carry HIV into the brain, where the virus can infect immune-like cells called microglia. Gradually antibodies and killer cells bring the infection under control, and the amount of virus drops.

In many viral diseases, that would be the end of the story. The immune defenses would mop up the remaining virus. Copies of the antibodies and sensitized killer cells would be kept in the immune system's "memory" to be mobilized against any new attack by the same kind of virus. In AIDS, however, though the body wins this battle, it is only the first round in a long, drawn-out fight.

HIV has many weapons in its fight for survival. First of

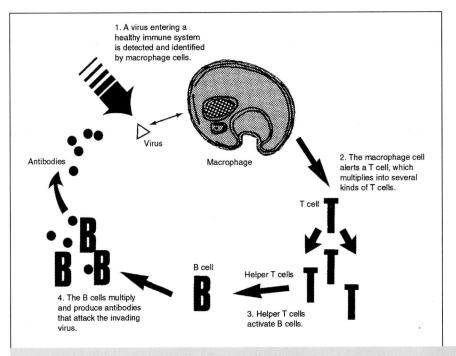

1. A virus entering a healthy immune system is detected and identified by macrophage cells.

Virus

Antibodies

Macrophage

2. The macrophage cell alerts a T cell, which multiplies into several kinds of T cells.

T cell

B cell

Helper T cells

4. The B cells multiply and produce antibodies that attack the invading virus.

3. Helper T cells activate B cells.

The immune system: Macrophages, T cells, and B cells cooperate to defend the body against invading germs.

all, each time new virus particles are produced, the HIV RNA must be copied. Reproduction of our genes and those of other animals includes careful proofreading and editing of the genetic information to catch and correct any copying errors that occur. The AIDS virus lacks such a correction process, and many errors are made in copying its RNA. That might not sound like an advantage, but it is. Individual virus particles are cheap. It is estimated that during the average ten-year period after infection, when nothing much seems to be happening, actually close to 2 billion helper T cells are being produced and destroyed each day, and the virus passes through up to five thousand generations, producing at least one trillion virions.[13] The copy errors produce inheritable changes, or mutations, in the virus. Most of the mutations do not make much difference or are harmful to the virus, making it unable to reproduce or to infect new host cells. But a few mutations result in slightly different proteins on the surface of the virion. These viruses may not be recognized by the body's defenses, and they can then multiply unhindered until new antibodies or killer cells are found to match them.

It is a constant race between the immune defenses and the virus, but one in which the body's defenders have a handicap. Helper T cells, which play key roles in the production of antibodies and killer T cells and help coordinate the efforts of the macrophages, are attacked and killed. Moreover, by binding to the CD4 proteins on the T cells, HIV can stop them from working even if they are not actually infected. The body tries to compensate by producing more immune cells, but there is a lot of wasted effort. Some of the new cells target forms of the virus that have already been replaced by mutated HIV.

Each time the immune system is mobilized to fight some other invading germ, the T cells and macrophages are activated, and HIV reproduces faster. Eventually the immune defenses are depleted, and opportunistic infections develop. It is these infections, rather than the direct effects of HIV itself, that may ultimately kill a person with AIDS.

How AIDS Spreads

Tennis great Arthur Ashe died of AIDS, acquired from blood transfusions during heart surgery. Indiana teenager Ryan White had the hereditary blood disease hemophilia and developed AIDS after receiving HIV-contaminated blood products. His poignant story became so familiar to Americans in the late 1980s that the first law providing federal assistance for the care of AIDS patients, passed by Congress in 1990, was named in his honor. In the early years of the AIDS epidemic, blood transfusions and blood products for hemophilia caused thousands of cases of AIDS. In the

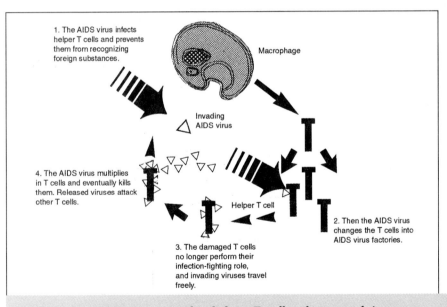

1. The AIDS virus infects helper T cells and prevents them from recognizing foreign substances.

Macrophage

Invading AIDS virus

4. The AIDS virus multiplies in T cells and eventually kills them. Released viruses attack other T cells.

Helper T cell

2. Then the AIDS virus changes the T cells into AIDS virus factories.

3. The damaged T cells no longer perform their infection-fighting role, and invading viruses travel freely.

When the AIDS virus invades helper T cells, the normal immune defenses break down.

developing nations, contaminated blood can still be a problem; but in the United States and other industrialized nations, the blood supply is now almost completely safe. Since 1985, all blood donations have been tested for antibodies to HIV, and those that test positive are discarded. The processing of blood products used to treat hemophilia has also been modified to remove or kill any viruses that might be present, and synthetic clotting factors have now replaced some natural blood products. It is estimated that one out of every 450,000 to 660,000 blood donations is HIV-contaminated and may pass through blood-screening tests undetected. Since an average blood transfusion requires five or more units of blood, a person's risk of receiving infected blood in a transfusion is one in 83,000 to one in 122,000.[14]

There is another way that contaminated blood can transmit HIV. When users of injected drugs share needles and syringes, traces of blood from one user may be drawn up into the needle. These traces may then be transferred to another user who injects drugs into a vein, using the same needle and syringe. (Flushing the needle and syringe with diluted household bleach kills any HIV that may be on them.) It has been estimated that about one third of the AIDS cases in the United States were due to infections transmitted through the use of injected drugs.[15] People who have become infected with HIV by using contaminated needles may then pass the virus on to their sex partners. Needles used for tattooing or body piercing can also transmit virus-contaminated blood if they are not sterilized carefully between each use.

The main way that HIV is spread is through sexual contact. Seminal fluid and other body secretions of an infected person contain HIV, which can be transferred to the person's sex partner. Anal intercourse is the most dangerous because the lining of the rectum is very thin. Cuts or tears

She shows all the signs of having HIV.

There aren't any you can see. You just can't tell from outward appearance who is infected with HIV, the virus that causes AIDS. To determine your risk for HIV and AIDS, call your State or local AIDS hotline. Or call the National AIDS Hotline at 1-800-342-AIDS. Call 1-800-243-7889 (TTY) for deaf access.

  U.S. DEPARTMENT OF HEALTH & HUMAN SERVICES / Public Health Service CDC HIV is the virus that causes AIDS. AMERICA RESPONDS TO AIDS

☆ U.S. GOVERNMENT PRINTING OFFICE 1998—634-984

may develop, allowing the virus to get into the receptive partner's bloodstream. HIV can also directly infect cells of the rectal lining, later moving into the blood. Vaginal intercourse can also transmit HIV infection and is the main route for the spread of AIDS throughout most of the world. Transmission from infected males to females is much easier, but a man can be infected by contact with vaginal secretions of an infected woman. In oral sex, the virus in secretions from the vagina or penis may be transferred to an uninfected partner through cuts or sores in his or her mouth. HIV has also been found in saliva, so there is a theoretical possibility of transmission from mouth to penis or vagina, but there have been no reliably documented cases. Infection by other sexually transmitted diseases such as chlamydia, gonorrhea, and herpes makes the transmission of HIV more likely in two ways. Open sores allow HIV to penetrate into the bloodstream, and the inflamed tissues of people with active STDs secrete increased amounts of HIV.[16]

Researchers Norman Hearst and Stephen Hulley of the University of California, San Francisco, have calculated that the odds of becoming infected by a single act of heterosexual intercourse range from one in five hundred when the male partner is HIV positive and no condom is used to one in 50 million when the partner is of unknown HIV status and is not in any high-risk group and a condom is used. Having multiple sex partners or repeated sexual contact with an infected partner raises the odds dramatically. The odds of infection in five hundred sexual encounters with an HIV-infected partner, for example, are two in three when condoms are not used; for five hundred unprotected sexual contacts with partners of unknown status who are in a high-risk group, the odds of becoming infected are one in three.[17] Contrary to some common beliefs, a person *can* become infected in his or her first sexual experience; and having a partner who looks clean and healthy is no guarantee of safety. People in the early stages of HIV infection who have no symptoms of AIDS can pass the virus to sex partners.

HIV can be transmitted by a mother to her baby before or during birth, and also by breast-feeding. Children infected in the womb test positive for HIV antibodies and develop AIDS more rapidly, usually showing symptoms during the first year of life. (However, not all children born with HIV antibodies are actually infected; some of them just received antibodies from their mothers, not the virus. These antibodies later disappear, and the children no longer test positive.) Children infected during delivery do not test positive for HIV until four to six months of age and progress to AIDS much more slowly. Studies have shown that mothers with a higher viral load (the amount of virus in the blood and tissues) are more likely to transmit the virus to their babies. An infected woman who breast-feeds has about a 14 percent risk of transmitting HIV to her child. If she first becomes infected during the months she is breast-feeding, the risk increases to 29 percent. In developed countries, HIV-positive women are advised not to breast-feed, but in developing countries where adequate nutrition and good health care may be difficult to obtain, breast-feeding is still recommended.[18]

HIV is *not* transmitted by casual contact—shaking hands, sharing towels, or eating food prepared by someone who is HIV-infected. Family members do not "catch" HIV by daily contact with someone who has AIDS. There have even been cases of identical twins, one born infected and the other HIV negative, who have slept in the same crib and shared toys and bottles without the second twin becoming infected.

Opportunistic Infections

We all carry around germs on and in our bodies. Normally they just live quietly, using us for food and shelter but not

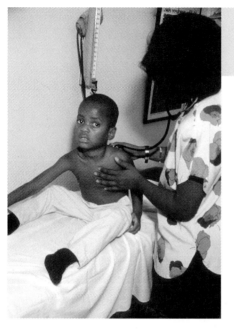

A child infected with the AIDS virus is examined at a medical center in Haiti.

doing any real harm. Our bodies' immune defenses help keep them in check. People with AIDS, however, have defective immune defenses that provide an *opportunity* for normally harmless germs to cause trouble. About 90 percent of AIDS-related deaths are caused by opportunistic infections. Among the rest, 7 percent are due to cancer and the other 3 percent to miscellaneous causes. People with AIDS typically develop a variety of opportunistic infections, not just one. The particular mix depends to some degree on where the patient lives and the person's financial resources. People in developing nations, for example, tend to develop bacterial and protozoal infections that are not usually found in wealthier countries, where sanitation is better and there are more medical resources for antibiotics and clinical care.

Toxoplasmosis is a parasitic disease that does develop in AIDS patients in the United States. The protozoan that causes it, *Toxoplasma gondii*, is found in cats and dogs; a pet owner may become infected while changing a cat's litter box. Ordinarily this parasite causes only a mild illness, if any, although in pregnant women there is a danger of birth defects. In someone infected with HIV, toxoplasma can infect the brain or damage the retinas of the eyes, resulting in

Some People Are Immune to AIDS

As the AIDS epidemic developed, there were scattered reports of people who did not become infected despite continuing sexual contact with an infected partner. There were also reports of people who were HIV positive but went on year after year without developing any symptoms or even any drop in the numbers of disease-fighting cells. A group of researchers headed by Anthony S. Fauci, director of the National Institute of Allergy and Infectious Diseases (NIAID) and chief of NIAID's Laboratory of Immunoregulation, has been studying a group of HIV-infected people and their sex partners since the early years of the epidemic. Some people (as many as one percent of the white population) have a genetic mutation that prevents the body from forming one of the receptors HIV needs to invade CD4 cells. So, even after years of exposure to the virus, people with this gene may never become HIV positive, or they may develop AIDS much more slowly than is usual. The researchers believe that not only the people's heredity but also the particular strain of HIV they are carrying and various other factors help determine whether AIDS will develop. Infection by other diseases can also influence progression to AIDS by activating the immune system and making its cells more vulnerable to HIV.[19]

blindness. Other protozoans can damage the lining of the stomach and intestine.

In someone with a damaged immune system, yeastlike fungi can cause thrush, producing whitish growths and sores in the mouth and throat, as well as infections of the vagina and rectum. Other fungi can cause meningitis (inflammation of the membranes covering the brain and spinal cord) and pneumonia (such as PCP, caused by *Pneumocystis carinii*).

Tuberculosis (TB), a bacterial disease that seemed to be well under control in the general population, has recently been making a comeback. The bacterium that causes it, *Mycobacterium tuberculosis*, is fairly common, but under modern conditions the body can usually bring it under control. After a TB infection is fought off, the bacteria are not completely destroyed. Instead, the bacteria may be closed up inside small, round swellings in the lungs called tubercles. If the immune defenses are lowered, TB can become reactivated and may occur not only in the lungs but in various other parts of the body. There are effective antibiotics for treating TB, but they must be taken for months, which requires a lot of cooperation from the patient. Many people with AIDS and TB are homeless or too ill to cope; they may stop the treatment before it is completed. When this happens, drug-resistant bacteria may develop, and these may be transmitted to healthy people.

Various herpesviruses can cause trouble in people with AIDS. Herpes simplex infections can be activated when immune defenses are low. Cytomegalovirus (CMV), another member of the herpes family, can cause brain infections, retinitis, pneumonia, and gastrointestinal infections in immune-deficient people. Epstein-Barr virus, which causes mononucleosis in healthy young adults, can produce cancers in the immune-suppressed. Varicella zoster virus (VZV), which causes chickenpox, can later reactivate as shingles, an excruciatingly painful rash.

AIDS Can Affect the Brain and Nerves

Between 55 and 65 percent of AIDS patients develop progressive dementia (mental deterioration), which starts with forgetfulness, loss of the ability to concentrate, slowness of thought, slurring of speech, loss of balance, and impaired motor function. In about 10 percent of adult AIDS patients, these are the first symptoms of AIDS; however, they usually occur after other symptoms have developed. AIDS dementia may progress to loss of speech, muscle weakness, and eventually headaches, seizures, coma, and death. The early stages may be hard to diagnose because these symptoms are similar to those of depression, which often develops in people with AIDS.[20]

4

Diagnosing AIDS

Fifteen-year-old Robert R. had come to Washington University Hospital in St. Louis complaining of pain and swelling in his legs and genitals. His lymph nodes were very swollen, and an examination showed he had chlamydia, one of the most common sexually transmitted diseases. Microbiologist Memory Elvin-Lewis, a chlamydia expert, was called in to consult. The doctors prescribed antibiotics, put Robert on a low-salt diet, and wrapped and elevated his legs to help reduce the swelling. However, the treatments did not seem to help. Over the next fifteen months, Robert kept getting sicker. His muscles wasted away, and he was gasping for breath as his lungs filled with fluid. After he died of

46

pneumonia, in May 1969, an autopsy revealed that he had also had Kaposi's sarcoma. This assortment of ailments would be quickly diagnosed by doctors today, but back in 1969 it was a complete puzzle. In fact, Elvin-Lewis asked that some of the tissue specimens be deep-frozen so that they could be examined later if new knowledge might help clear up the mystery.

As Elvin-Lewis raised her own young children and worked as a microbiologist, she was haunted by the sad story of Robert R. In the 1980s she was intrigued by the reports of a new disease that seemed strikingly similar to Robert's problems, and she wrote up the case in medical journals, speculating that it might have been AIDS. She planned to have the frozen tissues reexamined as soon as better tests were developed. In 1985 she nearly lost her chance. She had accompanied her botanist husband, Walter, on a field trip to the Amazon basin. While she was gone, her lab was remodeled; two of the freezers were plugged into faulty outlets, and half of the specimens she had collected from interesting patients were destroyed. Two other freezers were okay, though—including the one containing Robert's tissues. Meanwhile, another of Robert's doctors, Marlys Witte, then a surgery professor at the University of Arizona, had requested the tissue samples for testing. In 1987, tests of the tissues proved that Robert had indeed been one of the first people with AIDS in the United States.[1]

Today, tests for antibodies to HIV are more commonly used to screen blood and organ donations and to determine whether people who have engaged in risky behavior have been infected by HIV. Actually, like Magic Johnson, people often find out their HIV status indirectly—when a test is run on blood they have donated or as part of routine tests to qualify for an insurance policy or a job. Kaye B., for example, had a lifelong dream of a military career. But when the high school senior from Houston, Texas, tried to enlist in the

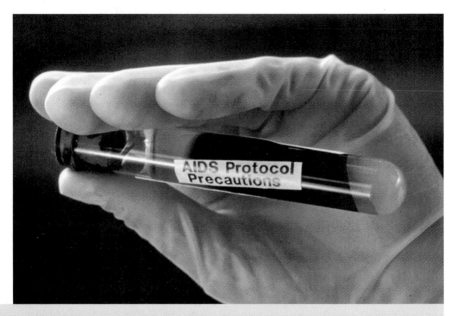

Patients often discover their HIV status when their blood is sampled for a routine test.

army, she received a certified letter asking her to report to the processing station to discuss the results of her medical examination. The letter said she had a "potentially serious condition of a personal nature." Kaye was shocked to learn that her blood test was HIV positive. She was offered a retest to make sure the result was correct, some information about HIV and AIDS, and a list of specialists she could go to. Kaye's recruiter gave her personal counseling to help her get over the shock and later kept in touch with her to check on how she was coping. Meanwhile, Kaye spoke to the boys with whom she had had unprotected sex and advised them all to be tested for HIV infection. She believed that whoever transmitted the virus to her did not know at the time that he was infected. "Then after I got tested," she speculated, "he went and found out he was positive and was too embarrassed to tell me."[2]

Antibody Tests

The first HIV test developed, and the one still most often used, is the ELISA (*e*nzyme-*l*inked *i*mmuno-*s*orbent *a*ssay). HIV-1 (the most common form of the virus) is grown on cultured human cells, and antigens (substances that react with antibodies) are isolated from it. The antigens are then bound to a solid surface—either glass beads or small wells in a glass or plastic plate. A patient's serum (the liquid part of blood, containing dissolved proteins) is applied to the HIV-coated beads or wells and left for an hour to react. After the serum is washed off, the coated surfaces are treated with chemical reagents. If the patient's blood contains antibodies that bind to the test antigen, they form a complex and produce a characteristic color.

Questions about the accuracy of the test can usually be cleared up either by repeating it or by using a more complicated and expensive test called the Western blot test. Experience shows that when these tests are performed by an experienced technician, confirmed positive results are about 99.8 percent accurate, and negative results are virtually 100 percent accurate. The development of semiautomated versions of the ELISA test has helped eliminate possible errors due to the work of inexperienced technicians. The ELISA test takes about four hours and costs from seven dollars in state-sponsored laboratories up to seventy-five dollars in private laboratories. Western blot tests take 12 to 24 hours and are more expensive but also more specific than ELISA. Tests for antibodies to HIV-2 (a less-common, milder strain of the virus) have also been available since 1990, but they are routinely used only for blood screening.

There are some problems with these tests. They are not

really tests for AIDS, but rather for HIV infection, and they test for antibodies to HIV, not the virus itself.

False positive results (that is, a positive test result when the blood sample does not contain HIV antibodies) can occur because the tests were made extremely sensitive. They were designed for screening donated blood rather than for testing people. The developers of the test logically felt that if there was any question about the results, it was safer to just throw out a suspect blood sample than to take the chance of transmitting the virus during a blood transfusion. False positive results are perhaps due to the presence of antigens that happen to resemble those that develop with HIV. Although they do not matter much in blood screening, a false diagnosis of HIV infection on the basis of such a test can ruin a person's life. People have sued for and won financial compensation after living in constant fear for years and suffering from side effects of powerful drugs given on the basis of an incorrect diagnosis.

False negative results can also occur. Usually they are not the fault of the tests themselves, but the result of taking the test during the window just after infection, when the body is battling the virus but has not yet made enough antibodies to show up in the tests. Antibodies may be detectable two weeks after infection, but for most people they take longer to develop. Studies have shown that about 90 percent of HIV-infected people seroconvert (that is, produce measurable antibodies to HIV) within three months, and a small percentage take a year or more.

In the immunofluorescent antibody test, a known preparation of antibodies labeled with a fluorescent dye is used to test for either antigens or antibodies in a person's blood. Versions such as Fluorognost are highly accurate and fast enough to do in a doctor's office (about ninety minutes). The Recombigen latex agglutination test can be used on blood serum, plasma, or whole blood. The sample is mixed

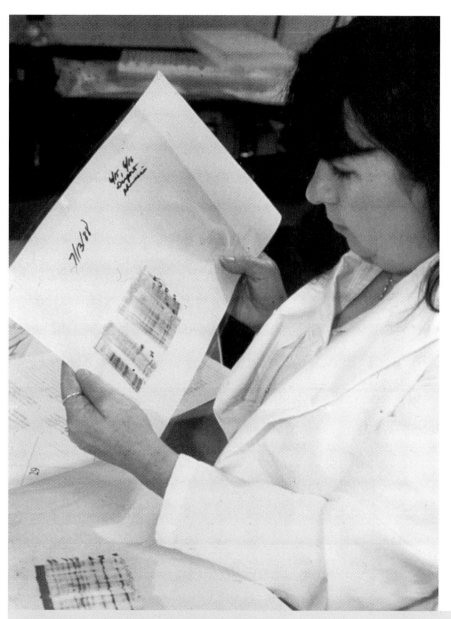

A technician interprets Western blot test results. The test is used to determine if a blood sample contains HIV.

with a suspension of tiny latex beads coated with HIV antigens and placed on a card together with positive and negative controls. The test takes just five minutes and requires no special equipment.

Antibody tests have also been developed for samples of urine, saliva, and cells from the inner lining of the cheek. Such tests can be more convenient for screening under field conditions. People may be more willing to take a test that does not require collecting blood; health workers are protected from accidental infection by needle sticks; and in developing countries where there may not be resources available for sterilization or throwaway tools for collecting blood samples, the danger of spreading infection during testing is minimized.[3]

Tests for HIV

In 1989 the FDA licensed HIVAG-1, the first diagnostic kit to detect the presence of the actual virus rather than antibodies to it. HIVAG-1 tests for key virus proteins. It can detect infection earlier than the antibody tests. Other tests for the virus use gene probes, chains of DNA that home in on portions of the virus's genes that have been copied in the form of DNA and attached to chromosomes in the white blood cells. The probe uses a radioactive tag that can be spotted by test instruments. A technique called PCR (polymerase chain reaction) is used to multiply the extremely small amounts of nucleic acid in a virus gene into about a million copies so that it can be detected more easily. Nonradioactive versions of PCR tests have also been developed. The PCR tests have helped reveal the kinds of cells infected by HIV and the intense viral activity that goes on during what medical researchers formerly believed was a latent period, before the appearance of symptoms. They are also used in determining the viral load—the amount of virus present in the blood. Doctors use this information to predict which patients are likely to progress to AIDS and to monitor the course of their treatment.[4]

The Ethics of AIDS Testing

Should a person whose blood has been tested for AIDS antibodies at a blood donation center be told the results of the test? Should the blood of patients admitted to a hospital for surgery or treatment for some other ailment be routinely tested for HIV infection? If so, who has the right to know the results, and should they be entered on the patient's medical records? Should newborns be routinely tested for HIV antibodies, and should their mothers be told the results? Can someone be forced to take an HIV test?

These are questions that have been debated ever since the first tests for HIV antibodies were developed, and there are legitimate arguments for both sides. Public health agencies do not routinely screen large numbers of people for HIV infection, as they do for other sexually transmitted diseases. In twenty-five states, doctors are required to report the names of their infected patients. However, in most places

Teen Rights

In general, people under the age of eighteen have the right to counseling, testing, and treatment for sexually transmitted diseases without the consent or knowledge of their parents. However, some states do not classify AIDS as a sexually transmitted disease. As of 1997, sixteen states had passed laws specifically guaranteeing the rights of teenagers to get testing for HIV without having to get a parent's or guardian's permission.[5]

people can get tested anonymously. AIDS advocates have battled to keep test results confidential, arguing that revealing the results could lead to harmful discrimination against people who are already suffering in their fight against illness.[6]

In 1996, an effort by some members of Congress to require HIV testing of newborns was turned aside in favor of voluntary testing of pregnant women.[7] In certain circumstances, however, courts have held that some considerations are more important than confidentiality. In 1997, for example, the New Jersey State Supreme Court ruled unanimously that a rape victim could demand that her convicted attackers be tested for HIV infection, simply for the sake of her peace of mind, and that she should be notified of the results.[8]

It might seem that the ultimate in HIV test confidentiality would be a do-it-yourself home test kit. Several companies have developed such kits, but for a long time the FDA was reluctant to approve one. The administration's concern was not for the accuracy of the results, but for the need for counseling to accompany the results of a test for HIV infection. Two home test kits for HIV antibodies, Confide and Home Access Express-HIV Test, were finally approved in 1996. They are actually compromises: The person uses a disposable tool called a lancet to prick his or her finger and places three drops of blood on a test card with an identification code. The card is then mailed to the laboratory, which runs the test and repeats it if it is positive. The person calls the laboratory after a week and punches in the identification number from the card to get the result. No name, address, or other identifying information is submitted, so the result remains anonymous. Callers whose tests were positive or uncertain are connected to a counselor who explains the results and refers the person to a local doctor or health clinic. A counselor is also available to speak

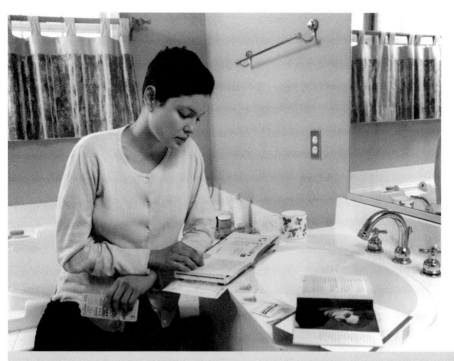

Testing for the HIV infection can be done at home, using simple test kits.

with people who had a negative result but have further questions or concerns.[9]

In 1997 the CDC reported that, based on data collected from the states, about two thirds of the estimated 775,000 Americans infected with HIV have been tested and know their status. (This estimate does not include the people who have been tested anonymously.) However, the other third of those who are HIV positive are not receiving the early treatments that might help control the disease.[10]

5

Treating AIDS

I'm excited. I feel strong. I feel hopeful. I feel normal again." In 1994, Eduardo Torreau would not have expected to be making those comments to an interviewer from the *Wall Street Journal* for a feature article in mid-1996. He had spent four months in the hospital, fighting for his life as TB and pneumonia threatened to overpower his crippled immune defenses. But then he was admitted to an experimental program testing a combination of a new drug, a protease inhibitor, with two older anti-AIDS drugs, AZT and 3TC. After twenty months on the drug cocktail, Torreau had gained thirty-five pounds of muscle and was actively making plans for the future. A former dancer, the thirty-nine-year-old New Yorker had just begun taking courses to prepare for a new career in computer graphics.[1]

Others interviewed for the article also felt as if a death sentence had been cancelled. The previous October, twenty-nine-year-old Californian Andrew Howard had taken a "last vacation" to Hawaii, where he and his companion, Charles Bouley, spread the ashes of a friend who had died of AIDS. When they returned, Howard was so weak he could barely get out of bed. He suffered from fever and dizziness and had lost so much weight that he was literally wasting away. He gave his companion the power of attorney; he no longer felt up to dealing with legal matters. "Andy's spirit had broken," says Bouley. Then, in November, Howard was accepted into a clinical trial of a new drug combination being held at Stanford University. In just four weeks he began to feel better as his symptoms disappeared. By June he had gained fifty pounds, was working out at a gym each day, and had hired an agent for the screenplays he was writing. "I feel wonderful, incredible," he said. "I hope it lasts."[2]

A flurry of cautiously optimistic reports in June 1996 about the use of new drug combinations in the treatment of AIDS swelled to an excited chorus at the AIDS conference in Vancouver, British Columbia, in July. Some researchers even hinted that a cure might be possible. "I am doing experiments trying to see whether HIV can be eradicated," said virologist David Ho.[3] It was hoped that if the virus could be stopped from reproducing, eventually all the infected cells would die off as they were replaced by new cells. Then the therapy could be stopped; the patient would be cured. Further experience in treating AIDS patients with combined drug therapies over the months that followed, however, dampened some of the early enthusiasm. It was discovered that even when the treatments seemed to be working well, HIV survived among the genes of resting T cells. If a new infection prompted these T cells to start dividing again, the virus would soon be producing new HIV virions and causing trouble all over again. HIV could also remain in hiding in other nondividing body cells, such as the nerve cells in the brain. These cells would be a reservoir from which the virus might later emerge, reactivating the disease.[4]

The Long Road to Progress

For years after AIDS first came to the attention of the medical and health care community, no one was sure what was weakening the patients' immune systems. Therefore, the only thing doctors could do for the patients was try to treat the opportunistic infections as they cropped up. Drugs such as pentamidine and trimethoprim-sulfamethoxazole, for example, stop *Pneumocystis carinii* from reproducing. They were used to treat PCP and prevent it from recurring. Ganciclovir was used to treat CMV retinitis, and other drugs were given for various fungal infections. Genetically engineered interferon (a protein that normal cells produce when they are infected by a virus) was approved for the treatment of Kaposi's sarcoma. All these drugs had serious side effects, however, and some patients could not tolerate them. Moreover, the patients' immune systems were so severely suppressed that one opportunistic infection after another kept cropping up.

After it was discovered that HIV was the cause of AIDS, researchers hunted for drugs that might kill the virus or stop it from causing so much damage. The first drug developed that was actually targeted to HIV itself was AZT (an abbreviation for *azidothymidine*; it was later renamed zidovudine). Marketed starting in 1987 under the brand name Retrovir, it remained the only drug against AIDS available for the next four years.

Scientists refer to AZT as a reverse transcriptase

A pharmacist uses a pill counter to fill a prescription for an AIDS drug.

inhibitor. AZT is very toxic; its side effects include severe damage to the blood-forming cells in the bone marrow, resulting in anemia (a severe drop in the number of red blood cells, which carry oxygen to the body cells). Moreover, within months or even weeks, the virus in the patient's body can become resistant to the drug. This happens because mutations are constantly appearing in the virus population. Some of the mutants are able to get around AZT's effects, and those multiply rapidly. As a result, though AZT treatments made the patients feel better for a while, the effects were only temporary.

The next anti-HIV drugs to be developed were four more reverse transcriptase (RT) inhibitors, approved by the FDA in 1991 and the following few years. Like AZT, they are nucleoside analogs; that is, they are chemically similar enough to the natural nucleic acid building blocks to be mistakenly picked up; they then stop the gene-building process. Other RT inhibitors, approved in 1996, are not nucleoside analogs. They work by changing the shape of RT so that it will not fit the building blocks. The new RT inhibitors are somewhat more effective than AZT and have milder side effects, but they are still far from ideal.[5]

Meanwhile, researchers were working on drugs to attack other links in the chain of events by which HIV invades a cell. By 1998, four drugs of a different type had won FDA approval for the treatment of AIDS: protease inhibitors, which tie up an HIV enzyme called protease. This enzyme cuts a long protein chain into a number of smaller pieces that the AIDS virus needs in order to grow.[6]

At first, as new drugs were added to the stock of weapons against AIDS, doctors started with one drug, then switched to another when the virus built up resistance. However, Dr. David Ho, who was one of the first researchers to demonstrate that HIV actually reproduces rapidly soon after infection, had a different idea. He suggested hitting the

Have a HAART

After years of experience in using drugs against HIV, AIDS experts now believe that the best way to bring the infection under control is HAART: highly active antiretroviral treatment. Several drugs are used at once to attack the virus, reducing its numbers and stopping it from dividing to prevent mutations to resistant forms from developing. Usually a combination of two nucleoside analogs and one or two protease inhibitors are used. As of 1998, the lineup of FDA-approved drugs included:[7]

RT inhibitors (nucleoside analogs): didanosine (ddl, Videx); lamivudine (3TC, Epivir); stavudine (d4T, Zerit); zalcitabine (ddC, Hivid); zidovudine (AZT, Retrovir).

RT inhibitors (non-nucleoside analogs): delavirdine (Rescriptor); nevirapine (Viramune).

Protease inhibitors: indinavir (Crixivan); nelfinavir (Viracept); ritonavir (Norvir); saquinavir (Invirase and Fortovase).

Nearly all these drugs, however, may have unpleasant or even dangerous side effects, and many pills must be taken on a very complicated schedule. Drug companies are developing combined pills to simplify the treatments and help patients take them properly.

virus simultaneously with several drugs as early as possible after infection, before the viral load had time to build up. Although no single drug could completely stop HIV from reproducing, several drugs working in different ways might do the job—and the virus would not be able to become resistant to all of them at once.

Researchers were skeptical at first, but the results with drug cocktails were impressive. Immune functions were at least partly restored, and the viral load was greatly reduced or even became undetectable. Subsequent studies showed that the drug cocktails also wiped out HIV hiding in the lymph nodes.[8]

Hope for Some, Disappointment for Others

For the first time, the new drug cocktails provided hope of converting AIDS from a fatal disease to a chronic condition, like diabetes, that could be managed while still living a relatively normal life. *Time* magazine named David Ho as the Man of the Year for 1996.[9]

As more months passed, however, the news turned into a mixed message. Many of the patients taking the drug combinations continued to thrive. There were even scattered reports of patients who had stopped taking the drugs after their viral load became undetectable and still remained apparently HIV-free up to a year or more later.[10] In about half the patients, however, the drug combinations did not work or could not be tolerated, or after a long period of

restored health the virus suddenly returned and the T-cell counts fell again. The protease inhibitors could produce serious side effects. Drug-resistant HIV strains presented a growing problem, requiring doctors to work out by trial and error the best drug combination for each patient.[11]

AIDS researcher Dr. David Ho was named Time *magazine's Man of the Year in 1996.*

When Should Treatment Be Started?

Magic Johnson decided to start taking anti-HIV drugs soon after he first learned he was HIV positive. For him, so far, the treatment has been a great success. But many people do not respond as well.

Doctors believe that the best time to start treatment is right after a person gets infected. The virus will not have had time to multiply very many times or to cause much damage, and prompt treatment could wipe it out completely. Unfortunately, however, most people do not realize at first that they have been infected. Many do not have the flulike early symptoms (or they may think they have the flu), and tests will not detect the virus early on. Another obvious time to start treatments is when patients begin having symptoms or when tests show that their CD4 cell count falls below 200 per cubic millimeter. Without treatment, their lives are in danger. Current guidelines recommend starting treatment when the viral load reaches 10,000 per cubic millimeter. However, a 1998 study showed that since AIDS may progress more rapidly in women, it might be advisable to start their treatment at a viral load of 5,000.[12]

Federal guidelines for treatment, published in June 1997, recommended the use of three drugs, including two nucleoside analogs and a protease inhibitor. "If you make the decision to treat," commented Dr. John Bartlett, cochairman of the Panel on Clinical Practices for the Treatment of HIV Infection that drew up the guidelines, "it should be an aggressive attack on the virus." He noted that about 60 percent of those who know they are infected with HIV and are under a doctor's care are currently taking protease inhibitors.[13]

Some patients who are responding well to the new therapy find themselves almost afraid to hope. "I had a date when I knew I was going to die, and now all of a sudden I'm going to be allowed to live for a while longer. Who knows how much longer? . . . Obviously I don't know. I do know that instead of being overjoyed, I feel like I'm being jerked around," remarked one counseling client. It is a terribly frustrating time for the people who have not been helped by the new treatments, while they know or read about others who have almost literally come back from the dead to start planning for the future again. "I don't like to whine," said one of these patients to his counselor, "but it is really difficult hearing all the good news and how these drugs have heralded the end of the plague. . . . It's very lonely not being able to talk to other people about what it's like hearing all the good news and feeling totally left out."[14]

It is even more frustrating for the majority of HIV-positive people, who may never have the opportunity to try the drug cocktails. The treatments are extremely expensive, costing up to $20,000 a year, and a patient must take as many as twenty pills throughout each day in a complicated sequence. Some pills must be taken on an empty stomach, others with meals; and they may interact with drugs taken for other conditions, such as TB or cancer. Skipping doses can allow resistant strains of HIV to appear, and the resistance then may be passed on to others, making their treatment more difficult as well. Many people, including the working poor in the United States and virtually everyone in the developing nations, cannot afford the treatments. Federal funds are available to help with treatment costs, but there is not enough money to go around. Doctors also tend not to prescribe the complicated combination treatments to people who are not likely to stay on the rigid schedules required. Some homeless people and drug addicts cannot cope with ordinary daily living; how could they keep up with the complicated AIDS treatments? Even those who would be willing to try cannot control the circumstances of their lives. Where does a homeless person put a drug that has to be refrigerated? How does someone who depends on soup kitchens for meals maintain a low-fat diet and eat at strictly regular times? Treatment does not seem practical under such conditions, and yet the idea of denying treatment to some while allowing others to benefit is troubling to many health care workers.[15] "It could well become a major ethical issue if, as a matter of course, for example, we don't offer these drugs to poor people, people of color or people with substance abuse problems," says Dr. Paul Volberding, AIDS specialist and professor of medicine at the University of California, San Francisco. Daniel Baxter of Casa Promesa, an AIDS residential treatment center in Bronx, New York, warns that fears that patients might not keep to the treatment plan could be used as an excuse for discriminating against "marginalized people—the ones we avert our eyes from on the street."[16]

Living with AIDS

HIV-positive people taking drug cocktails find themselves coping with some unexpected problems. First, there are the complexities of juggling schedules and remembering to take all the right pills at the right time. Having to take so many pills is also a constant reminder that they are battling HIV, which requires some hard psychological adjustments. Drug manufacturers are developing combination pills that will make things a bit simpler. The first one, Combivir, a combination of AZT and 3TC, was approved by the FDA in the fall of 1997. Ironically on the same day of its approval, a report was published saying that patients taking three-drug combinations without AZT did just as well as those whose drug cocktails included AZT, and they experienced fewer side effects.[17] A further advance came in 1998, with the approval of Sustiva, which can be taken in just one pill a day. Combined with nucleoside analogs or a nucleoside analog and a protease inhibitor, the use of Sustiva can allow people with AIDS to control the virus with as few as five pills a day.[18]

AIDS patients taking drug cocktails must still cope with side effects, such as diarrhea, muscle spasms, and anemia. If the patient sticks it out, these may subside after a few months. And then there are money problems. Health insurance may not pay for new drugs. The federally funded AIDS Drug Assistance Program provides at least partial help, but it is administered by the states, which may severely limit the treatments that are covered. Some of the drug companies have been helping by donating drugs for those who cannot afford them, or continuing treatment for the patients who participated in clinical trials while the drugs were being developed. Financial woes are further compounded for some people with AIDS who did not expect to survive. They cashed in their life insurance, maxed out their credit cards, and indulged in some "last wishes"—never dreaming that they would still be around when the bills came due.[19]

One troubling result of all the hopeful stories in the media about advances in treating AIDS is that many people have been getting the mistaken impression that there is now a cure. Comments twenty-year-old Manuel Sanchez, a coordinator at a New York City organization serving gay, lesbian, and bisexual youth, "So it's like, 'O.K., so I don't have to worry. You know, there's a cure for it.' . . . and the young person is just going to go out there and have unprotected sex."[20] In fact, however, preventing infection is still the most effective way to keep the AIDS epidemic in check.

AIDS Babies Growing Up

Thirteen-year-old Johnny and eleven-year-old Marie and Donna are chatting and snacking on potato chips at a table in a Bronx, New York, medical building. They first met in preschool day care, and now they attend weekly meetings at a support group. Like a growing number of others, they were infected with HIV before birth. They have all gone through numerous medical crises that sent them to the hospital—"Like 2,000," giggles Marie—and have taken anti-HIV drugs. They live with the emotional realities of AIDS, too. Each is an orphan, living with a grandparent or in an adopted family. They all know about their condition, although they sometimes find it hard to understand. (Johnny resents the fact that his two older siblings do not have AIDS; Marie insists that her mother could not have died of AIDS because "AIDS was not invented yet.") They keep it a secret from friends, classmates, and even family members for fear of being judged a bad person. Soon they, like a growing number of AIDS babies, will have to make decisions about sexual activity.

At the support group meetings, the friends trade practical tips, rehearse what to do in various situations (Donna decided to use "Ask my mommy" as her answer to questions about a two-week stay in the hospital), and speculate on what heaven is like. When asked what they want to be when they grow up, Donna says she wants to be a dancer and Marie a nurse; but Johnny just shakes his head. "I never think about it," he says.[21]

6

Preventing AIDS

Henry Nicols was born with hemophilia and contracted HIV at the age of eleven. When he was seventeen years old, he developed AIDS. At age nineteen, he and his sister, Jennifer, had spoken about AIDS at 150 high schools, colleges, and community centers in twenty-three states.

Jennifer usually begins the presentation with a single question: "Does anyone know what someone with AIDS looks like?" People shrug their shoulders. Then she'll say, "Well, right now, most people in this country who are infected with HIV look just like you." During the introduction, Henry hides in the audience, waiting for his sister's cue. Then Jennifer describes her brother as someone

If You're Dabbling In Drugs... You Could Be Dabbling With Your Life.

Skin popping, on occasion, seems a lot safer than mainlining. Right? You ask yourself: What can happen? Well, a lot can happen. That's because there's a new game in town. It's called AIDS. So far there are no winners. If you share needles, you're at risk. All it takes is one exposure to the AIDS virus and you've just dabbled your life away.

For more information about AIDS, call 1-800-342-AIDS.

 U.S. DEPARTMENT OF HEALTH AND HUMAN SERVICES / Public Health Service who has AIDS and calls him up on stage. The audience is stunned, with some thinking: "I was sitting right next to him, and I had no idea." People often get the idea that a person with AIDS has to look sick. Jennifer explains that people may not know whether their boyfriend or girlfriend is infected. She then emphasizes that this uncertainty is why it is so important for people to protect themselves.

During the presentation, Henry and Jennifer spend time answering questions about AIDS and clear up any misconceptions or myths. They also suggest that anyone who feels he or she might have been infected should be tested. People often think, "Why bother? If you're positive, you're going to get AIDS and die anyway." But not knowing could be dangerous—you could infect someone else. In addition, there are drugs to treat AIDS. Therefore, the earlier you find out, the better your chances of living a longer and healthier life.

At the end of the presentation, Jennifer tells everyone that any decision they make now could affect the rest of their lives. "My brother is nineteen, and the doctors say that he is dying. He's a good brother and a basically good kid, but none of that matters, because people with AIDS die." Then she adds, "Within the next ten years, everybody in this room will lose somebody they love to AIDS. The only difference between your family and ours is that we already know who that person is going to be."[1]

Jennifer and Henry have made a strong impression in the young minds of thousands of people throughout the nation. They have helped get the message across that although there is not yet a cure for AIDS, it is a preventable disease. There are simple, practical, and effective things people can do to avoid becoming infected by the virus that causes it. HIV is transmitted mainly by unprotected sexual activity and through the sharing of needles by users of injected drugs. Abstinence—both from sexual activity and from injection

Miss America
Speaks Out

Kate Shindle, Miss America 1998, made it her mission to educate young people about HIV and AIDS. "We have within our power the ability to stop HIV in its tracks. The answer is prevention," she stated in her platform, and she devoted her year as Miss America to helping in this goal. Visiting schools and youth groups across the nation, she provided straight talk and frank answers to touchy questions. She urged young people to educate themselves about HIV and AIDS by reading printed and Internet materials and talking to people who know. "Examine your own behaviors and be honest," she advised. "Talking about sexual issues is never easy, but it's nothing to be ashamed of, especially when your own life and others' are involved." Getting tested if you think you might have been exposed to HIV, getting treated if you are HIV positive, and protecting yourself by not engaging in risky behaviors were key points in her message. "Don't be afraid to say NO," she emphasized. "Don't ever let others pressure you into sex or drug use, no matter how much you care about them. It's your body and your life!" Miss America advised young people to respect others rather than judge their lifestyles. She also urged them to become part of the solution by helping to educate family and friends about HIV and volunteering in a local HIV prevention program.[2]

Kate Shindle, Miss America 1998, helps educate young people about the dangers of HIV.

drug use—is the only *absolutely sure* way to avoid HIV infection through these routes. But in some situations, complete abstinence may not seem like a practical choice. Measures such as the use of condoms during sexual activity can help reduce the risk of infection. There are also things that people who face special risks at work—such as health care workers who may come in contact with virus-contaminated blood—can do to minimize their danger. In each case, education is important. Learning the facts about what activities are risky and how to cut down the risks is a necessary first step to staying safe from AIDS.

AIDS Education in Public Schools

Education plays an important role in the fight against AIDS. In New York City, for example, AIDS education was mandated in every school in 1987. However, there had been an ongoing debate over when and what children should be taught about AIDS. A curriculum adopted in 1992 called for emphasis on abstinence as the best way to protect against the transmission of HIV. It specified that the teaching of AIDS information should start early and be age-appropriate. For instance, lessons in kindergarten through third grade would teach how diseases are transmitted and introduce AIDS as a disease that—unlike a cold—is hard to catch.[3] Critics complained that this AIDS education policy did not give all the important information about how to protect against HIV transmission. "The new rules will enable the board to censor or ban materials that they think fail to stress abstinence,"[4] said Schools Chancellor Joseph A. Fernandez. He was later fired after starting a controversial program of demonstrating the proper use of condoms in sex education classes in the public high schools and making them available, free, to students.

Political pressures have prompted the United States

Congress and various local legislators and school boards to stress educational programs promoting abstinence and sometimes to forbid the teaching of any alternatives. And yet, say AIDS researchers Thomas J. Coates and Chris Collins, "abstinence-only programs do a disservice to America's youth."[5] The researchers say that a single message does not work for everyone, and educational approaches need to be specially designed to fit the needs of

Protect Yourself!

Many young people are doing volunteer work in outreach programs that go into the neighborhoods to provide information on sex and AIDS. Effective education includes not only instructions on the use of condoms and other safer-sex techniques but also tips on how to make them work in real life. Even people who know better may allow themselves to be pressured into having unprotected sex because insisting on condoms seems like too much of a hassle, or it is embarrassing to talk about, or it seems as though they do not trust their partner. It may sometimes seem hard to say no to risky behavior like unprotected sex or experimenting with drugs, but not saying no may mean giving up a long healthy life for a few minutes of pleasure. It is best to start talking about things like safe sex right up front, before things start getting hot. Remember that loving someone means caring about what happens to that person. Someone who tries to pressure you into doing things that could hurt you does not really care about you. You are better off getting out of such a relationship, no matter how painful that might seem.[6]

LAST WEEK, CLASS, WE LEARNED ABOUT HEARING AIDS. TODAY WE'RE GOING TO TALK ABOUT BAND-AIDS...

GLASBERGEN

Wanting to avoid controversy, Mr. Jackson approached AIDS education slowly and cautiously.

people of different ethnic and cultural backgrounds, age groups, and sexual preferences.

This view is supported by a number of studies. One experiment, for example, was conducted on 659 sixth and seventh graders in inner-city Philadelphia schools. Three groups each received eight hours of health education aimed at preventing the spread of HIV. The teachers of one group stressed abstinence, another group learned about the use of condoms, and a third, a control group, received general instructions on avoiding diseases. When questioned three months after the lessons, only 12.5 percent of the students in the abstinence-only group reported having sex recently, compared with 16.6 percent of the condom group and 21.5 percent of the controls. But six months and a year after the instruction program, fewer members of the condom group reported recent sexual activity, and the percentage among the abstinence group was rising closer to that of the controls. Moreover, those in the abstinence group were more likely to have engaged in unprotected sex. Apparently after some time of living in the "real world," the message had worn off for the students who had been told only about abstinence. Those who had learned about the use of condoms had received practical information they could use in their own lives. "If the goal is reduction of unprotected sexual intercourse, the safer-sex strategy may hold the most promise, particularly with those adolescents who are already sexually experienced," the researchers noted in

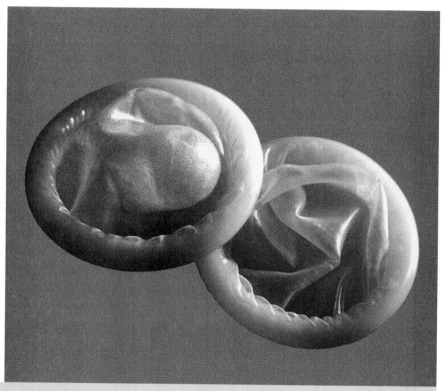

If your partner doesn't have a condom, you just have to take a deep breath and go get one.

their report in the *Journal of the American Medical Association.*[7]

A United Nations-sponsored review of sixty-eight reports from a number of different countries also found that sex education programs do not result in an increase in sexual activity among young people. On the contrary, young people who have been taught the facts about sex and HIV infection tend to have their first sexual experiences later, have fewer sex partners, and have fewer unplanned pregnancies and sexually transmitted diseases.[8]

Condoms Can Reduce the Spread of HIV

Laboratory experiments have demonstrated that using latex condoms can be a very effective method for preventing the transmission of HIV. In these studies, condoms were filled with fluids containing HIV. The results consistently showed that the virus did not penetrate the latex.[9] Condoms are not foolproof because they can break, tear, or slip off. The percentage of condom breakage is actually very low, however—equal to or less than 2 percent. If the condom does break, it is usually because of user error, not condom quality. One cause of condom tearing is the use of petroleum jelly or mineral-oil-based lubricants, which eat away at latex. To be most effective in AIDS prevention, condoms should be used with a water-based lubricant that contains nonoxynol-9, a spermicide that also destroys the AIDS virus. If used correctly, condoms can be a highly effective form of protection against AIDS and other sexually transmitted diseases.[10]

Children of HIV-Infected Mothers Are at Risk

In 1994 it was estimated that seven thousand HIV-infected American women gave birth each year, and 25 percent of those babies were HIV positive. There is now hope for children born to HIV-infected mothers. A study sponsored

The Vaginal Pouch

Manufacturers have produced a new type of condom: a female version of the male condom. The FDA approved the female condom, also called the vaginal pouch, in May 1993, and it has become available to the general public. Many men do not like to wear condoms and often choose not to use them. The female condom gives women the power to protect themselves from AIDS and other sexually transmitted diseases. However, male condoms are still the best protection against disease.[11]

by the National Institutes of Health (NIH) showed that taking the drug AZT can significantly reduce the risk of mother-to-child transmission of HIV. Trials included 477 pregnant HIV-infected women. During pregnancy and labor, these women received either AZT or a placebo, a harmless fake pill that looked like the real thing but did not contain the active drug. (Neither the women nor their doctors knew beforehand who got which pills.) After birth, the babies received the same drug as their mothers for six weeks after delivery. Tests of 364 infants revealed that AZT greatly reduced the risk of mother-to-child transmission. Only 8.3 percent were likely to become HIV-infected if they and their mothers received AZT, compared with 25.5 percent of those who did not get the drug.[12]

AZT treatment has now become standard for HIV-infected pregnant women in the United States and other wealthy nations, but the cost (about a thousand dollars per woman) is far too high to be practical in Third World countries. And yet, according to UN estimates, one thousand HIV-infected children are born throughout the world each day.

Occupational Hazard

Health care workers have always understood that their job entails a certain degree of risk: They are in constant contact with patients, or their blood or other body fluids. But since the AIDS epidemic began, *occupational hazard* has taken on a whole new meaning. Many health care workers take care of HIV-infected patients every day. Their risk of becoming HIV infected through exposure at work is more significant than risks in any other environment. However, the chance of infection has been greatly reduced since the CDC required that all health care workers follow standard infection control procedures, commonly known as universal precautions. These safety practices include hand washing; wearing wrap-around smocks, gloves, and masks; careful handling of needles and other sharp instruments; and strict sterilization procedures. In addition, health care workers are required to use universal precautions in all situations even if there seems to be no risk, because there is no way of knowing who is actually infected.

Universal precautions have undoubtedly cut the risk of accidental transmission of HIV, as well as of other germs. However, latex gloves may not provide health workers with total protection from accidental needle sticks while they give shots or set up IVs. If the needle stick is deep enough, it can penetrate protective gloves and draw blood. In the United States, an estimated 250,000 to one million health care workers are stuck with needles or other sharp instruments each year. However, from the beginning of the epidemic up to early 1998, only fifty-two infections of health care workers by HIV had been documented as resulting from exposure at work; there were also 114 possible other cases.

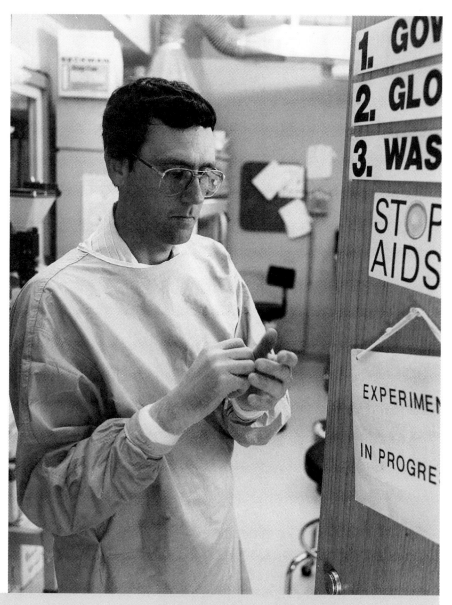

An AIDS researcher at the NIAID Laboratory of Immunoregulation puts on gloves, part of the recommended procedure for those working with the AIDS virus.

Twenty-four of the documented cases and 58 of the possibles had developed AIDS. Although the total is relatively low—especially when compared with the seven thousand health care workers who are infected with hepatitis on the job each year—the risk is very real and the consequences are very frightening.[13] But now there is hope for health care workers. A 1995 study revealed that the drug AZT can dramatically reduce the risk of infection with the AIDS virus for health workers who are accidentally stuck with needles or other sharp instruments.[14]

Clean Needles Reduce the Spread of HIV

Intravenous drug users are responsible for a large portion of the HIV-infected population. In 1993, New York City had an estimated two hundred thousand drug users and half of them were infected with HIV.[15] Nationally, of the more than five hundred thousand AIDS cases diagnosed since 1981, about one third were caused by the use of injected drugs.[16]

HIV is spread when drug users share needles. During injection of the drug, the IV drug user typically draws some blood into the syringe to make sure the needle is inserted into a vein; if the syringe is then used by someone else before it is carefully washed and disinfected, this blood may be injected into another drug user.[15] Most states make it illegal for anyone to have hypodermic needles and syringes without a doctor's prescription. Therefore, with sterilized equipment hard to obtain, drug users feel they have no choice but to share their needles and syringes. Addicts often go to "shooting galleries," which are apartments or alleyways where they pay a small fee to get privacy and a needle to use. Unfortunately, these needles are usually contaminated from a previous use. If the needles are contaminated, then the AIDS virus can be transmitted from one drug user to another. The drug users can then pass it on to sexual partners and even to their offspring.

In 1985 Dr. David Sencer, New York City health commissioner, believed that the fight against the spread of AIDS should be focused on intravenous drug users because they account for such a large proportion of HIV infections in the United States. He proposed that needles be sold over the counter to help cut down the danger of shared needles. Needle-exchange programs had been tried successfully in places such as the Netherlands, where automatic dispensing machines that exchange a fresh needle for a used one were installed. But in New York, Sencer's suggestion was rejected by the city's mayor, district attorneys, and the National Institute on Drug Abuse.[18]

In 1988, Yolanda Serrano, the head of a private

AIDS Delaware outreach case managers hand out condoms and bleach kits on a Wilmington street corner.

addiction and AIDS prevention organization in New York City called Adapt, or the Association for Drug Abuse Prevention and Treatment, shocked authorities when she devised a program that involved distributing clean needles and syringes to drug addicts in exchange for their contaminated ones. Although Serrano's plan was against the law, she fought for it, and the first municipal needle-exchange program in New York was finally started by the New York City Department of Health.

The needle-exchange program was often located outside a storefront or a parked van, or it was mobile, where the van roamed the streets or the workers walked around looking for drug addicts. The fixed locations also offered other services such as HIV testing and counseling, TB testing, or condom distribution. The needle-exchange program was anonymous. Addicts could go to inconspicuous locations and exchange their contaminated needles for an equal number of sterile ones.

The needle-exchange program faced a lot of controversy. Mayor David Dinkins banned the program in 1990, shortly after he got into office. He felt that it was sending out the wrong message, telling drug addicts that it was okay to use drugs. Serrano was determined to see her plan succeed and defied the law by continuing to give clean needles to addicts; the police rarely interfered.[19] However, Dinkins later changed his view of the needle-exchange program and decided to legalize it in 1992.[20]

In October 1993, a seven-hundred-page California study on the effectiveness of the needle-exchange programs was released. The study concluded that the programs probably decreased the rate of HIV infections, and there was no evidence that they increased the amount of drug use in the communities they served.[21] In another study, during the period from 1988, when the first needle-exchange program was started, to 1992, the needle-exchange program in Tacoma, Washington, held the rate of HIV infection among

IV drug users to only 5 percent. In New York City, where only a few programs were operating during that time, the proportion of HIV-infected drug users rose from 10 percent to 50 percent.[22] Needle-exchange programs have been set up since then in communities throughout the nation. By the beginning of 1998, more than one hundred needle-exchange programs were operating in seventy-one cities and twenty-eight states in the United States, exchanging about 8 to 9 million syringes each year.[23]

Some states still make it unlawful for drug users to possess needles and syringes, forcing needle-exchange programs to operate illegally. One of these is New Jersey. In 1996, two people attempting to start up a needle-exchange program there were arrested; they were convicted and fined in 1997. Drug users account for 52 percent of all AIDS cases in New Jersey—the highest proportion in the nation.[24]

However, other states have increased their awareness about the programs. In 1992, for example, Connecticut passed a law that made it legal for pharmacies to sell needles and syringes. During the following five years, needle sharing decreased by 40 percent, the rate of HIV infection slowed, and injection drug use did not increase. Referrals to drug treatment centers increased, and the chief of police of New Haven, Connecticut, claimed that there had been a 20 percent drop in crime in the city, apparently due to the better relationship between city workers and the community.[25]

Another way to reduce HIV transmission through contaminated needles is to distribute bleach to drug users so that they can disinfect their needles themselves. However, using bleach is not very common on the streets, and many drug users do not follow the recommended procedures. Researchers need to try to devise a way to make sterilizing injection equipment easier and more effective than present techniques.[26]

7

AIDS and Society

During the 1988 Olympics, Olympic diver
Greg Louganis became the only man to win
gold medals at consecutive Olympics—four
gold medals in both the 1984 and 1988
Games. In June 1994, Louganis surprised the
nation at the Gay Games in New York when
he announced that he was homosexual. But in
February 1995, Louganis revealed even more
shocking news: He was infected with HIV. In
fact, he had known about his condition since
March 1988, five months before the Olympic
Games in Seoul.

   In 1982, Louganis became involved in a
relationship with a man he calls Tom.
Although he and Tom were a gay couple, it
was early on in the epidemic, and they never

talked about AIDS. But then Louganis got scared when some of Tom's friends got sick and died from complications of AIDS. In 1987, a former companion of Louganis, Kevin, wrote to him and informed him that he was HIV positive. (Kevin died three years later.) That summer, Tom developed shingles, a common infection in HIV cases. Louganis convinced himself that it had nothing to do with AIDS. "All around us gay men were getting sick, getting tested, getting educated, but we remained in denial." As Tom got weaker and weaker, it became apparent that he did indeed have AIDS. Louganis took an HIV test in March 1988 and found out that he was HIV positive. He did not tell anyone at first. Four weeks later, he finally told his coach, Ron O'Brien, and together they kept his secret.

During the preliminaries of the springboard event in the 1988 Olympic Games, the unthinkable happened. Louganis cracked his head on a reverse dive. He became "paralyzed with fear" when he started bleeding in the pool. Although he felt certain that the chlorinated water in the pool would dilute the blood and kill the virus, he was shaken. "I was so stunned," Louganis recalls. "I mean, what was going on in my mind at the time was, What's my responsibility? Do I say something? It's, you know, this has been an incredibly guarded secret." Louganis did not reveal his condition to the U.S. Olympic Committee doctor, who stitched up the wound without any protective gloves.

When O'Brien was asked if he was afraid that Louganis would infect someone else, the coach responded: "No, not really. Because there's very, very little chance. If it were a sport like boxing, wrestling, or football, where there's a lot of contact, but in the sport of diving, it is unlikely that Louganis would ever come into contact with anybody."

The U.S. Olympic Committee later adopted strict guidelines about the handling of athletes' blood, including rules that health workers and trainers use latex gloves.[1]

Right to Privacy

People with AIDS are often afraid to reveal their condition to the public for a variety of reasons. They fear that people's attitudes and behavior will suddenly change. Friends and acquaintances might no longer see the person as someone they have always known. He or she is a person with AIDS— a PWA. The PWA's whole life suddenly becomes threatened: job, school, playing sports, and even just hanging out with friends. It is understandable that someone would want to keep the condition a secret. Many people with AIDS continue to fight desperately for a right to privacy. But what

Diver Greg Louganis, gold medal winner in the 1984 and 1988 Olympic Games, announced that he was HIV positive in 1995.

happens when this secret threatens someone else's life? Did Greg Louganis have the right to privacy when he did not tell the attending physician about his condition?

The Bergalis Case

In September 1990, a famous Florida case challenged the HIV-infected person's right to privacy. Kimberly Bergalis, a young Florida woman, shocked the nation when she claimed that she had become infected with the AIDS virus after a routine visit with her dentist, Dr. David Acer, in December 1987. Dr. Acer, who was bisexual, had known about his condition since September 1987. He died in September 1990, shortly after he sent out a letter urging his former patients to be tested for HIV. Bergalis was one of six of his patients who had become infected with HIV.

When Bergalis first broke the news to the public, health officials quickly looked for other possible ways she could have become infected. But Kimberly and her family insisted that she had never had sex or used drugs. Finally, the Centers for Disease Control (CDC) in Atlanta discovered that her particular strain of HIV was almost identical to Dr. Acer's. Bergalis then wrote an angry letter blaming the state health officials for not protecting Dr. Acer's patients. She and her family started a crusade and demanded laws that would require mandatory HIV testing for health care workers and require that they tell patients about their condition.[2]

The news of the Bergalis case spread fear throughout the nation. This was proof that AIDS could infect anybody. It no longer targeted only certain groups of people. However, everyone seemed to be reacting with such strong emotions over Bergalis's situation and her crusade that the actual facts about transmission of the disease between doctors and patients were made to seem unimportant. Many health officials argued that mandatory testing would not give the community any additional protection against AIDS. The risk of being infected by a doctor "is so remote that it may never be measured," says former Surgeon General C. Everett Koop. "Since the epidemic started, 50,000 to 70,000 health professionals have become infected with HIV and have performed bloody, invasive surgical procedures on tens of millions of patients, and not one patient is known to have contracted HIV during such a procedure."[3] (After a thorough investigation, the CDC concluded that exactly how Dr. Acer's patients became infected may never be known; the most likely explanation was that the dental instruments became contaminated when the dentist's staff did some work on his own teeth and then the instruments were not sterilized properly.) It has been estimated that the chances of a patient being infected by an HIV-infected surgeon are about one tenth the risk of being struck by lightning and one fourth as likely as being killed by a bee.[4] On the other hand, health care workers are actually at far greater risk of becoming infected with HIV from their patients than the other way around. As of the beginning of 1998, there had already been fifty-two documented cases of such infections, and five of those health care workers had died.[5] As for HIV transmission from health care workers to patients, the Dr. Acer incident had been the only case reported as of 1998.

In April 1991, facts and figures did not seem to matter in the ruling by State Supreme Court Judge Philip S. Carchman in Mercer County, New Jersey. Carchman ruled that an HIV-infected surgeon must inform patients before performing surgery or any other invasive procedure. This became the first court ruling in the nation regarding which was more important: the protection of a health care worker's confidentiality or a patient's right to know.[6] Carchman felt that protecting a patient's life came first, no matter how minimal the risk. In accordance with this ruling, in July

1991 the CDC recommended mandatory testing for doctors and dentists and consideration of the results of the tests before they were allowed to perform certain procedures.[7]

However, new information about the risk of HIV transmission later prompted the CDC to eliminate some of their original recommendations, such as mandatory AIDS testing. In addition, the National Commission on AIDS declared that there was "no medical or scientific justification for restricting the practice of AIDS-infected health care professionals, nor should they be forced to tell their patients that they carry the virus." The commission also said that AIDS testing should be voluntary rather than mandatory. It concluded that the best way to prevent transmission of the AIDS virus in a health care environment was to follow the universal precautions. States have since been required to construct their own health policies that follow guidelines similar to those of the commission.[8]

In 1994, the New Jersey Health Department introduced a policy that overturned Judge Carchman's 1991 ruling. The New Jersey Health Department stated that HIV-infected doctors, dentists, nurses, and other health care workers do not have to tell their patients before treating them. Instead, health commissioner Len Fishman urged that these health care professionals take maximum precautions against the spread of blood-borne infections in treating all patients. In defense of this decision, Fishman remarked, "If we are going to test all health care workers, then I think there is a corresponding responsibility to test all patients. A society that tests all of its health care workers and all of its patients is not the kind of society that I think most of us want."[9]

Not Only a "Gay Disease"

In San Francisco, Los Angeles, and New York—the cities that were the first to feel the impact of the emerging AIDS epidemic—volunteer groups were quickly set up to help people with AIDS. These organizations provided educational materials, hot lines for counseling, and practical services like shopping for groceries and feeding pets to help people with AIDS cope with the chores of daily living. The original members of these groups were mostly homosexual men, who viewed the disease as a unique threat to the gay community. In fact, the nonprofit organization set up in New York City was called the Gay Men's Health Crisis (GMHC). As the disease began to affect more and more of the general population, however, these organizations became available for anyone who needed help, including heterosexuals.

One day a gay man found another man at the GMHC attractive and struck up a conversation with him. He became surprised when the second man, who was not gay, was appalled by his advances. The gay man demanded, "What are you doing here? This is my place. This is for me and people like me."[10] That is becoming less true with each passing year.

HIV infection is still prevalent among homosexuals, but intensive educational efforts have produced changes in behavior that have greatly lowered the infection rate among gay men. Meanwhile, the virus has spread widely into the general population, infecting heterosexual men, women, and even children, especially teenagers. Young people are now engaging in sex and experimenting with drugs at an earlier age than ever before, giving them a higher risk of becoming infected by HIV.

A Changing Public Image

The AIDS epidemic has made our society more tolerant about what is considered acceptable to talk about in public. The media at first had a cautious attitude toward reporting the facts about AIDS. They talked around the touchy

This seven-year-old boy with AIDS was kissed and blessed by Pope John Paul II in a large public meeting in San Francisco, trying to eliminate the fear and stigmatization associated with AIDS.

subjects instead of reporting them directly. With both sex and excretory functions being taboo subjects, how could they talk about something like anal intercourse? Intimate sexual contact became a popular catchphrase for the main way HIV is transmitted. Gradually, however, reporters realized that they were unintentionally helping to feed the AIDS panic. Because reports on television and in the popular press were not saying exactly how people become HIV-infected, the public was getting the mistaken impression that almost any kind of activity—even a kiss or a hug—could spread the deadly virus. As the epidemic spread, this reluctance to be forthright began to change.

Now, more and more, the facts about HIV, AIDS, and sex are being presented and discussed openly and without embarrassment. In fact, these days condom advertisements are more direct than ever before. One public service advertisement on television shows a condom leaping under the blankets to join a love making couple. In another, a young woman stops in the middle of a passionate embrace with her boyfriend to ask, "Did you bring it?" He tells her that he "forgot it." She replies, "Then forget it!" These ad campaigns aim to persuade young Americans to protect themselves against AIDS, either by using condoms every time they have sex or by abstaining from sex altogether. This approach is different from the 1980s, when condom use was hinted at by showing a young man pulling on a sock.[11] People are now able to freely discuss sex and condom use on television and radio and in newspapers and magazines. In addition, the subject of AIDS has been dealt with in the entertainment industry through talk shows, movies, and even soap operas.

The old attitudes have not faded away completely, however. When the Jacksonville *Florida Time Union* ran an article in June 1996 with the headline, "Study: Oral Sex Poses HIV Infection Risk," 124 angry readers phoned in to complain about the use of the words *oral sex*. A number of people cancelled their subscriptions.[12]

Blaming the Victims

Although AIDS awareness continues to grow, there are still many people with mistaken ideas about the disease. They regard AIDS as a disease of gay men and drug addicts, and they believe the victims are only getting what they deserve as punishment for their sins. Senator Jesse Helms of North Carolina, for example, has remarked about people with AIDS that it is "deliberate, disgusting, revolting conduct that has caused them to contract the deadly disease."[13]

The widespread publicity about the Kimberly Bergalis

case helped to feed the prejudices about people with HIV. Shortly before her death, Bergalis had some angry words to say about her fate: "I did nothing wrong. Yet I'm being made to suffer like this."[14] Throughout Bergalis's illness, she and her family tried to make it clear to the public that she was different from other people with AIDS—she was an "innocent victim." This angered other HIV-infected people. They felt as if they were "innocent victims" too—that no one deserved to get this terrible disease, no matter how it was contracted.

AIDS Discrimination

A misguided 1986 ruling by Assistant United States Attorney General Charles Cooper stated that an employer could legally discriminate against AIDS virus carriers as long as the hiring or firing decision was based on a fear that the person might spread the disease. However, this decision was overturned in 1987 when the Supreme Court ruled that laws forbidding discrimination against the handicapped also apply to people with contagious diseases. The specific ruling pertained to a schoolteacher with tuberculosis, but a footnote referred to other contagious diseases such as AIDS. These laws were designed to "ensure that handicapped individuals (including AIDS patients) are not denied jobs or other benefits because of the prejudiced attitudes or the ignorance of others."[15] In 1998 a new Supreme Court ruling extended the protection against discrimination to people who were infected with HIV even if they had not yet developed any symptoms of disease. The Court's decision stated that HIV infection qualified as a disability under the Americans with Disabilities Act because it limits a major life function, reproduction.[16]

Legal or not, discrimination against people with HIV happens all too often, in every aspect of their lives. While some hospital workers have cared for them with selfless devotion, others have refused to. People with HIV have been evicted from their homes and fired from their jobs. School boards have tried to keep children infected with HIV and even their uninfected family members from coming to school. Some friends and relatives have been sympathetic and supportive and have built a new loving closeness, but others have abandoned people with HIV and treated them like lepers.

People who shun those with HIV act out of fear and ignorance. Polls have shown that in spite of all the efforts to educate the public on the subject, many people still think you can be infected with HIV by sharing a drinking glass or towel or swimming pool. In 1993, Dr. Allan R. Brandt, a panel member of the National Research Council, commented, "Ten years ago, we were talking about quarantines, about isolating AIDS patients. Now, socially, AIDS patients have been quarantined, they have been isolated by their social inequity."[17] Unfortunately that is all too often still true.

A number of insurance companies refuse to insure people from the main AIDS risk groups, sometimes asking personal questions of friends or neighbors to determine whether a prospective policyholder is a homosexual or drug abuser. Now some of them are using HIV tests to screen out bad insurance risks. The companies do have a legitimate interest in reducing their risks of insuring people who are likely to die or become disabled within a short time; but nobody knows how quickly a particular person with a positive HIV antibody test will develop AIDS. Even without treatment, many people have remained healthy for ten years or more after infection. Several states passed laws barring the use of antibody testing for insurance applicants, but most such regulations were overturned by court rulings.

AIDS discrimination has also found its way into the

Making a Short Life Count

Ryan White, originally of Kokomo, Indiana, was a friendly, intelligent young teenager who looked like "the boy next door." In 1985 he was diagnosed with AIDS. He had become infected by HIV-contaminated blood products used to treat his hemophilia.

Ryan faced discrimination when he was barred from school and forced to get instruction at home over a telephone linkup with his classroom. The boy tried to understand what all the fuss was about. He was running a paper route, he said, and going all over the neighborhood, and nobody minded. So how was this so different from going to school?

Ryan's mother went to court to win permission for Ryan to attend regular classes. But parents of his schoolmates protested, and neighbors made life so unpleasant for the Whites that they moved in 1987, to Cicero, Indiana.

The new neighbors were friendlier, and Ryan liked his new high school, but his health began to deteriorate. Before Ryan died of AIDS at age eighteen, in 1990, he became a national spokesperson for people with AIDS, recognized by nearly all Americans from his frequent appearances on TV shows and in photos in newspapers and magazines. "Sometimes when I go in his room, I break down completely, and some days I kind of smile at all the things he got to do and how happy he was," said his mother, Jeanne. She set up a memorial fund in Ryan's name at an Indianapolis hospital the day after his death and continued his mission as spokesperson. "*Everyone* is an innocent victim of this disease," she declared.[18]

workplace. Some employers have tried to require tests of employees or prospective employees. A Dallas, Texas, energy firm began requiring food service employees and applicants for these jobs to be tested for HIV antibodies in 1985, after a worker in the executive dining room was hospitalized with the disease. U.S. Public Health Service guidelines state, however, that there is no reason for routine screening of health care personnel, food handlers, or personal-service workers. In New Jersey, the Bedminster Township Board of Education announced a plan to screen teachers and staff for drug use and HIV antibodies. Such moves have been strongly opposed by civil liberties groups. The protests have won considerable support from the public, and the Bedminster school board dropped the plan for a testing program.

Ryan White's return to school became a widely covered media event.

America's largest employer, the United States armed forces, has set up a program to screen both recruits and current personnel for HIV antibodies. Recruits with a positive test are rejected. Current personnel who test positive are allowed to stay in the service but cannot serve overseas.[19] In January 1996, President Bill Clinton agreed to sign a bill that would require the Pentagon to discharge troops infected with HIV even if they are healthy and able. And yet, because the military tests troops regularly, the virus is detected early, long before AIDS symptoms develop and a person's abilities begin to diminish. Gay rights groups and civil liberties activists see this new policy as a clear case of discrimination: The military restricts the duty of about four thousand other troops who suffer from chronic but not debilitating illnesses, such as heart disease, cancer, and asthma, but does not dismiss them. The law was promptly appealed in the courts.[20] By the end of 1997, the question was still unresolved. Meanwhile there were more than one thousand people in the military who had become HIV positive while they were serving.[21]

Ironically, the discharge of HIV-infected military personnel would bring a unique line of AIDS research to a halt. Defense Department researchers were among the first to note the spread of AIDS into the heterosexual community, as the virus was transmitted to spouses and children. Through frequent testing and close health monitoring, researchers followed the disease at every stage of its development in thousands of patients. After discharge, the patients would disperse and be much more difficult to keep track of—even if there were non–Defense Department funding for such a project. Dr. Kenneth F. Wagner, research physician and retired Navy captain, calls the AIDS data compiled by the military a "national treasure" that is "irreplaceable."[22]

AIDS as a Weapon

Twenty-five states in the United States have an AIDS criminal law stating that it is a misdemeanor or felony for an HIV-positive person to deliberately expose others to the virus through methods ranging from sexual contact to the splattering of blood. Several other states that do not have specific AIDS criminal laws prosecute under laws against homicide and assault. By 1993, more than three hundred HIV-positive people had been prosecuted under AIDS criminal laws, and twenty had been convicted.[23]

In November 1993, in a case involving two homosexual lovers, United States District Court Judge H. Lee Sarokin ruled that "persons who conceal the fact that they have AIDS from their lovers should be held liable for injuries suffered by the unsuspecting partners—even if those partners do not contract the disease." Sarokin believed that "those who knowingly put others at risk should not escape liability merely by the fortuitous circumstances that their conduct did not result in the actual transmittal of the disease." This ruling proved similar to the case involving movie star Rock Hudson, who died of AIDS in 1985. Hudson's lover, Marc Christian, sued the star's estate after his death, claiming that Hudson had kept his condition from him. This case established a person's rights to sue for damages under these circumstances.[24]

In 1989, Gregory Dean Smith, a prisoner infected with the AIDS virus, bit a prison guard with the intent to cause harm. Smith was then prosecuted for attempted murder and convicted, adding twenty-five years to his sentence. After an appeal, the defense was still unable to prove that HIV cannot be spread through a bite. According to the trial judge, John B. Mariano of superior court, "Impossibility is not a defense to the charge of attempted murder. That is because our law, our criminal statutes, punish conduct based on state of mind. It punishes purposeful actions regardless of whether the result can be accomplished." In another case, prisoner Curtis Weeks was convicted of attempted murder when he spit on a guard because he wanted to "take someone out" with him.[25] Since then, transmission of HIV through a bite actually has been established in a few cases, but the virus was transmitted by blood, not saliva—the biter had bleeding gums. In a case where infection was found to result from deep kissing, blood was also the means of transmission; both partners had gum disease at the time.[26]

Activists Push Drug Approval

Since the beginning of the epidemic, AIDS has fired up the energies of the gay community in America. Effective organizations that educate the public and that care for people with AIDS, such as the Gay Men's Health Crisis in New York City and Project Inform in San Francisco, have been established. Many people with AIDS quickly became medically knowledgeable, and they equally quickly became frustrated with the way things were usually done in medical research. In the early years, a diagnosis of AIDS often meant that the person had at most a year or two left to live. The development and testing of new drugs typically took about twelve years from discovery through lab and clinical tests to FDA approval for marketing. People whose friends and loved ones were dying all around them found this schedule unacceptable. Their efforts brought about major changes in medical research and development.

People with AIDS and the primary care physicians who treated them got together to design community-based drug trials, instead of waiting for drug companies and government medical agencies to plan and implement them. Researchers at San Francisco General Hospital formed the

County Community Consortium (CCC) in 1985 and started a program in which doctors would distribute experimental drugs, monitor the patients, and collect data as part of their regular clinical work. Before this, studies had been done on a much smaller scale and had to be carefully analyzed and approved by the FDA before drugs could be distributed to broader groups of patients. "We have a distinct advantage in being able to follow up patients, because the research is being done where the patients are getting their primary care," commented Dr. Donald Abrams, the head of the CCC. He noted that even if patients dropped out of a particular study, their doctors were still aware of what ultimately happened to them.[27] In New York City, people with AIDS and activist doctors founded the Community Research Initiative (CRI) in 1987. CRI soon had a number of contracts for testing new AIDS drugs for various drug companies. "Traditional researchers thought that community doctors would not be sophisticated enough to run trials," recalls Mathilde Krim of the American Foundation for AIDS Research (AmFAR), a philanthropic organization that has provided major funding for AIDS research. "But actually they were highly sophisticated. . . . After all, they had been managing the disease for years."[28]

The community-based initiatives greatly accelerated the approval of new drugs. For example, in February 1987, NIAID researchers decided that using inhaled pentamidine aerosols to prevent PCP was a high priority. The researchers then spent more than a year formulating and writing a testing plan and negotiating with Lymphomed, the manufacturer of the product, before they even started looking for a group of patients to test in June of 1988. Meanwhile, the CCC and CRI began community tests of the drug in May 1987. Just two years later, after a careful examination of the data from the community programs, the FDA approved the use of the drug. This testing program also resolved another concern of the AIDS community: Different groups of patients received different doses of pentamidine, but no one was given a placebo. In its 1988 report, the Presidential Commission on the HIV Epidemic called for federal funding of the community-based research programs. A member of the commission described CRI as "one of the best things to have come out of the AIDS effort."[29]

Even the community-based research initiatives were not getting results fast enough to satisfy some members of the AIDS community. Larry Kramer, a gay playwright who had helped found the Gay Men's Health Crisis, later helped to organize a radical AIDS activist group called ACT UP (AIDS Coalition to Unleash Power). Specializing in confrontational, in-your-face politics and demonstrations designed to capture media attention, chapters of ACT UP in various parts of the world publicized such causes as lowering the price of AZT. ACT UP has organized marches on the FDA and on Wall Street, where stock trading in the major pharmaceutical companies takes place, to help speed up the FDA's drug-approval process. In the past, to get a new drug approved for marketing, the manufacturer first had to conduct detailed studies establishing that it was safe and effective, and then go through several years of FDA red tape involving the submission and review of thousands of pages of supporting data. Under pressure from AIDS activists, however, the FDA beefed up its fast-track processing of high-priority drug applications. In 1996, for example, it took just over ten weeks from NDA (new drug application) to FDA approval for the first protease inhibitor, and only six weeks for the second.[30] Steve Michael, chairman of the coordinating committee of ACT UP in Washington, D.C., commented, "If there were no ACT UP, there would be a million more deaths in this country. I know we've saved lives."[31]

AIDS activists have helped change the way medical research is done.

Quilt Brings AIDS Awareness

In 1987, the "names, pictures, and voices" of the men, women, and children who have died of AIDS were immortalized in the hearts of caring Americans through the patches of a huge, growing memorial quilt created under the sponsorship of the San Francisco NAMES Project. By October of 1988, when the quilt was displayed in front of the White House, it had grown to more than 8,000 three-by-six-foot panels and took up an area the size of seven and a half football fields. In 1993, the quilt had grown to more than 24,000 panels; and by 1997, to 45,000. Unfortunately, this reflects how rapidly the AIDS virus has been spreading in a short time.[32]

The NAMES Project views the quilt as a powerful educational tool. It shows people the diversity of lives that have been affected by the AIDS virus. People who have seen the quilt have been touched by its images. The quilt has changed many people's way of thinking about AIDS; some people have moved on to take positive action in their communities. One woman had this reaction to the quilt: "As much as you listen, as much as you see on television, as much as you read . . . to actually see and experience the quilt is the only thing that is going to shake a person's soul and allow them to reach out—to touch a place in their hearts that perhaps they didn't know existed."[33]

People who go to see the memorial quilt find the experience unique. They share a special emotional bond and find themselves coming together as a community. The quilt is a heartfelt tribute to AIDS victims.

8

The Future of
AIDS

Developing a new miracle drug can be a long and frustrating process. The protease enzyme of the AIDS virus was discovered in 1986, and drug company researchers immediately zeroed in on it as a potential target for stopping the disease. The first attempts to produce a protease-blocking drug, however, ran into difficulties. The compounds that worked in a test tube turned out to be too large to get into the bloodstream if they were taken in the form of a pill. By 1990 the drug companies had decided to try a different approach. Researchers at Pharmacia & Upjohn, for example, tested more than one hundred thousand different chemicals for activity against HIV protease. Some that worked, such as the rat poison warfarin, were too toxic—they might kill not only the virus but the patient as well. A joint venture by Merck and Du Pont produced a powerful protease inhibitor using computer-aided drug design, but human trials showed that the drug had dangerous side effects. Chemists at Abbott Laboratories produced one thousand possible drugs; three of them were promising enough for testing in humans. A number of drug companies, such as SmithKline, eventually gave up.

Knowledge, skill, and perseverance are key factors in the successful development of a new drug, but luck often plays a role, too. Norvir (ritonavir), the protease inhibitor that Abbott eventually put on the market, was the result of a chance meeting. Dr. David Ho had worked out a new theory about how AIDS develops. In 1991 he attended a conference in Florida, where Dr. Dale Kempf, a chemist at Abbott Laboratories, gave a talk about Abbott's experimental protease inhibitors. Dr. Ho thought the drugs might be good tools for testing his theory. Heading home after the conference, Dr. Ho found himself next to Dr. Kempf in the check-in line at the airport and told the Abbott chemist about his ideas. That conversation led to a joint research effort and a successful drug. Meanwhile, researchers at Merck were developing their own protease inhibitor, Crixivan (indinavir). The drug seemed promising at first, but then the virus began to multiply again—in every case except one. Patient 142, a forty-one-year-old law student, just "kept hanging in there and hanging in there," says Merck researcher Dr. Emilio Emini. When Merck officials met to discuss the future of the project in February 1994, it looked for a while as if it would be cut back. But Dr. Emini and others argued that the drug must be "doing something right" if it was keeping Patient 142 healthy. Finally, it was decided to expand the Crixivan test and try higher doses and combinations with other drugs. "If not for 142," says Dr. Emini, "it's possible we might have ditched the whole thing." As for Patient 142, in mid-1996, after nearly three years of Crixivan therapy, the HIV that he carried still had not developed resistance to the drug, and he had no trace of the virus in his bloodstream. "This is the most intensely satisfying experience of my life," the patient commented. "Maybe someday I can stand up in public and say I was the first person to conquer AIDS."[1]

New Targets

The reports of promising results with protease inhibitors and three-drug cocktails did not stop researchers from looking for new drugs with different ways of attacking HIV. This was just as well. As Dr. Steven Deeks of the University of California, San Francisco's public AIDS clinic at San Francisco General Hospital, noted at a conference in September 1997, "Over the past year, we had a honeymoon period. The epidemic will likely split in two [between those for whom the combination-drug treatments are effective and those who are not helped], and for half the people we will need new therapeutic options."[2]

Somewhat more encouraging news was reported at the Twelfth World AIDS Conference in Geneva in 1998. French researchers noted that the immune systems of some patients treated with the newest drug combinations slowly recovered. Eventually, patients who responded well might be able to discontinue the drugs when their own T cells were strong enough to keep any remaining HIV in check.[3] Other researchers reported that early drug treatment helped to preserve patients' helper T cells. Injections of an HIV vaccine called Remune, developed in the mid-1980s by polio vaccine pioneer Jonas Salk, were found to greatly increase the levels of helper T cells in patients taking drug cocktails. Reports at the conference emphasized, however, that the current multiple-drug treatments were a burden that many patients were unable to continue for the years needed to rebuild their immune defenses.[4]

Stopping HIV's First Step

Researchers are working on new drugs and therapies that target more than two dozen key steps in the life cycle of HIV. In the first step of the virus's attack, the HIV attaches itself to the cell's outer membrane. With the discovery that the virus needs to attach itself to two different receptors on the cell surface, both to the CD4 protein and to another such as CCR5, researchers had some concrete targets. If they could block the virus from attaching to its target cells, they could prevent infection. A soluble form of CD4, used to tie up the gp120 proteins on the surface of the virus, looked effective in test-tube experiments but proved disappointing when tried on AIDS patients. However, introducing a synthetic chemical called T-20 (pentafuside) dramatically reduced the viral load of HIV-infected mice in studies at the FDA antiviral lab in Bethesda, Maryland.[5]

Researchers at Wake Forest University have genetically changed white blood cells so that they do not produce the CCR5 receptor on their surface—like the blood cells of people with the natural mutation that makes them resistant to HIV infection. The experiment works in the test tube. Now the research team, headed by Si-Yi Chen, hopes to take white blood cells from AIDS patients, modify them, then inject them back into the patients' bloodstream to provide HIV-resistant immune defenses.[6]

Dr. John Rose and his colleagues at Yale University School of Medicine are using the new knowledge about the receptors HIV uses to attach to helper T cells in a different way. They have spliced genes for the CD4 antigen and another receptor, called CXCR4, into vesicular stomatitis virus (VSV), which infects cattle. This turns the cattle virus

Caught in the Act

In 1998, researchers at Columbia University and Dana-Farber Cancer Institute in Boston reported the results of an eight-year study of how HIV attacks a cell. Highly magnified X-ray pictures showed that first the HIV gp120 protein latches on to the CD4 protein of a lymphocyte. As CD4 pokes into a cavity in gp120, part of the HIV protein swings aside. A hidden pocket in gp120 opens up, and another HIV protein, gp41, pops out and harpoons the T cell's CCR5 protein. Only after it is firmly attached in both places can HIV's outer coat merge with the cell's outer membrane—the first step of infection. "When I first saw that," said Columbia University researcher Peter D. Kwong, referring to the cavity in gp120, "I said, 'That's the cure for AIDS.'" He believes that this spot will be a good target for drugs to stop HIV infection.[7]

into an AIDS-fighting virus hunter, which zeroes in on an HIV-infected cell and locks on to the gp120 antigens on its outer membrane. VSV then invades the cell and kills both it and the new HIV viruses forming inside it.[8] (The body soon replaces the killed T cells with new, virus-free cells.)

Tracking HIV Targets Step by Step

After fusing with the membrane of a white blood cell, HIV is "uncoated"; that is, the merging of the virus and cell membranes opens the way for the HIV RNA to move into the infected cell. A natural plant chemical, hypericin, produced by a shrub called St.-John's-wort, has shown some anti-HIV activity at this stage in animal tests. However, the low doses of St.-John's-wort sold in health food stores as an antidepressant are not effective against HIV.[9]

After uncoating, the virus directs the cell to make DNA copies of its RNA. This process is controlled by the enzyme reverse transcriptase, which was the target of the first successful anti-AIDS drugs. An anticancer drug called hydroxyurea can help make reverse transcriptase inhibitors more effective. Hydroxyurea blocks a cell enzyme that produces DNA building blocks. By decreasing the amount of normal building blocks available, the drug makes it easier for nucleoside analogs such as ddI to be taken up when the cell is building HIV genes. It also seems to help protect "resting" helper T cells, which are not dividing. Several patients who took hydroxyurea along with a drug cocktail

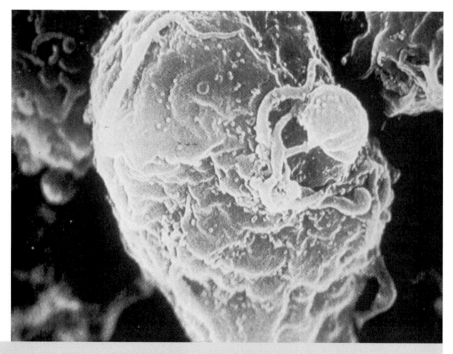

HIV buds out of a T-4 lymphocyte.

showed no signs of HIV reproduction even after they stopped the drug treatments.[10]

An enzyme called integrase, which attaches the DNA copies of HIV genes to the host cell's chromosomes, is the next big target for research efforts. A research team at the National Institute of Diabetes and Digestive and Kidney Diseases in Bethesda, Maryland, headed by Robert Craigie, has worked out the complete three-dimensional structure of HIV integrase and determined which part of it acts as the active site in incorporating the HIV genes into the host cell's DNA.[11] Meanwhile, several different groups of researchers are testing the activity of anti-integrase compounds on humans.[12]

The next steps in HIV's life cycle involve the production of RNA copies of the viral genes, which then direct the production of HIV proteins. Australian researchers are now testing ribozymes—RNA molecules that cut up the viral RNA so that it cannot form proteins—on six pairs of identical twins. One twin of each pair is HIV positive and the other is negative. The researchers take healthy lymphocytes from the uninfected twin and add genes to make ribozymes. Then they inject the lymphocytes into the HIV-positive twin in hopes of stopping the progression to AIDS. The ribozymes are designed to attack only HIV RNA, without harming any of the body's own RNA.[13]

Some of the HIV proteins are first produced in one long strand, which is cut into different-sized pieces by HIV's protease. The protease inhibitors work at this step.

An HIV protein called rev carries the HIV RNA out of the host cell's nucleus to direct the assembly of new HIV virions. Researchers are trying various antirev strategies, including decoy proteins, which attach to the RNA so that rev cannot get to them, and anti-rev antibodies, which tie up the viral rev so that it cannot carry the HIV RNA.[14]

Another approach to stopping the assembly of new

virions uses antisense RNA. This is an artificial form of RNA, constructed to bind to the HIV RNA. Antisense RNA covers the working parts of the viral genes and prevents them from forming new HIV particles. Researchers at Hybridon, a Massachusetts biotechnology company, have built an antisense molecule, GEM91, targeted against the HIV GAG gene. This gene directs the formation of the virus's outer shell, and its proteins are needed for the new virus particles to bud out of the host cell. According to Sudhir Agrawal, chief scientist at Hybridon, GEM91 completely stopped HIV reproduction in test-tube experiments. In contrast to AZT and other anti-AIDS drugs, it does not allow resistant strains of the virus to develop.[15]

Listening to the Body

Instead of focusing on HIV and potential weak spots in its life cycle, some AIDS researchers are looking at the natural

Keeping Ahead of HIV

The ability of the AIDS virus to mutate means that it can quickly produce new forms that are resistant to various drugs. If doctors could guess how the virus infecting a patient was going to change, they might be able to switch to a different combination of drugs that would be effective against the new mutants, too. Robert M. Lloyd, Jr., scientific director at Applied Sciences in Norcross, Georgia, has discovered that HIV goes through a series of changes on the way to becoming resistant to a drug. Tracking these changes would provide a crystal ball that could be used to predict what resistance the mutations were developing, giving scientists a chance to change to new drugs.[16]

substances in the body that keep the virus under control during the first stage of the infection. In particular, they are zeroing in on cytokines, the chemicals by which the various cells of the immune system communicate with each other and coordinate their activities.

One promising cytokine is interleukin-2 (IL-2), which signals the body to produce more T cells. Normally this substance, like the other cytokines, is produced in extremely tiny amounts. Using genetic engineering techniques, however, researchers have mass-produced IL-2 in bacterial cultures, and it is now available as a drug. In 1996 it was reported that, when combined with three-drug cocktails, IL-2 increased the number of CD4 cells in AIDS patients two- to fivefold, and at the time of the report the T-cell counts of five patients had remained at healthy levels for eighteen months after the IL-2 treatment was stopped. Using IL-2 to fight AIDS is very tricky. It has to be given by injection every two to four months over a five-day hospital stay, and it can cause very serious side effects, including fevers of 105 degrees Fahrenheit, severe nausea and vomiting, and leakage of fluid from the capillaries that can produce a life-threatening drop in blood pressure. It is also very expensive, costing about $3,000 to $5,000 a year.[17]

Several research teams have found other cytokines that may help keep HIV under control. A German research team headed by Dr. Reinhard Kurth claims that the active substance is interleukin-16, a substance produced by killer T cells that attracts helper T cells. Other researchers have focused on chemokines, a group of cytokines that activate white blood cells and direct their movements. An American group headed by Dr. Robert Gallo, now director of the Institute for Human Virology at the University of Maryland, says that a combination of three chemokines, RANTES, MIP-1-alpha, and MIP-1-beta, stop HIV from reproducing in test-tube experiments. These chemokines are produced in

A Controversial Experiment

Late in 1995, doctors at San Francisco General Hospital tried a desperate experiment: They transplanted bone marrow from a baboon into AIDS patient Jeff Getty. The theory was that, since baboons do not get AIDS, the transplant would provide HIV-resistant white blood cells that could help the patient fight the disease. The operation sparked a furious debate. Critics warned that the monkey might be carrying simian viruses that could not only be deadly for the patient but give rise to another epidemic. Both the fears and the hopes proved unjustified: Getty did not come down with any exotic monkey diseases, and the new bone marrow cells disappeared from his body after only two weeks. A year later, however, the patient was feeling much better. His chronic asthma, skin rashes, and lung infections had cleared up, and he had gained fifteen pounds of muscle. He had even completed a climb up his favorite 2,500-foot mountain trail. Getty and his doctors believe that his dramatic improvement was probably due to the radiation treatments he was given to prevent rejection of the transplant and to the protease inhibitors prescribed for him after the operation.[18]

the body at sites of inflammation and call in macrophages and other germ-fighting white blood cells. (MIP stands for *m*acrophage *i*nflammatory *p*rotein; RANTES comes from *r*egulated *u*pon *a*ctivation *n*ormally *T*-expressed and presumably *s*ecreted. "I made a horrible mistake," says Dr. Alan M. Krensky, who discovered RANTES. "I let my students name the molecule.")[19] Like the interleukins, these new chemokines can cause life-threatening complications if the doses are not exactly right. Moreover, Dr. Jay A. Levy of the University of California, San Francisco, who has been studying chemokines as potential AIDS drugs since 1986, believes that the active substance secreted by CD8 cells in HIV-positive people who have not developed symptoms is neither IL-16 nor the three inflammation chemokines found by the Gallo group, but another chemokine not yet identified. "At the very least," comments Dr. Anthony Fauci, head of NIAID, "the availability of . . . HIV-suppressive factors . . . will provide the framework for the development of strategies for therapy and vaccine development."[20] Identifying these chemokines, Dr. Fauci notes, "is very important and interesting, but we've been down this road before, and it's a majestic leap from the test tube to the human body."[21]

More Clues from Survivors

Back in 1980, a man in Sydney, Australia, donated blood to the Red Cross. Years later, public health officials learned that the blood donor had been HIV positive, and seven people who received transfusions of his blood became HIV-infected, too. But as the years went by, none of them—not even the original donor—developed AIDS. In 1995 a research team reported that the HIV strain that had infected this group of people was defective. Its gene for nef, one of the proteins that regulates HIV reproduction, was so abnormal that the virus could not reproduce efficiently. As a result, the immune systems of the infected people were able to keep the virus under control. Some of the people were found to have viral loads of as few as one or two copies of HIV per 100,000 T cells. The researchers speculate that this wimpy HIV may even act as a sort of natural vaccine that protects its carriers from more deadly strains of the virus.

The Australian finding also suggests that modifying the NEF gene (which carries the instructions for making the nef protein) might be one way to stimulate the immune defenses in people with AIDS. A form of HIV with a changed NEF gene could also be used to produce a vaccine that could protect people from becoming infected by the disease-causing virus. Experiments on monkeys conducted by Harvard University primate researcher Ronald C. Desrosiers support this view. Rhesus monkeys infected with SIV from which the NEF gene has been removed develop a low-grade infection but do not get the opportunistic infections typical of immune deficiency. Researchers at the University of Massachusetts Medical School in Worcester have also found a NEF defect in the HIV strain infecting a man with hemophilia who first tested HIV positive in 1983. Despite exposure to other strains of the virus until 1985, when routine screening of blood donations was started, the man did not become infected with a second strain and has not developed AIDS.[22]

Researchers at NIAID in Bethesda, Maryland, and at New York University School of Medicine in New York City have been studying some long-term nonprogressors (people who have gone many years after HIV infection without a major drop in their immune defenses or any symptoms of AIDS). The researchers have found that some people have inherited a resistance to the virus (such as those with a defective CCR5 receptor), while others apparently stay healthy because they have been infected by a weakened strain of HIV.

Other studies have focused on people who have remained HIV negative despite repeatedly engaging in unprotected sexual intercourse with HIV-positive partners. The majority of these people were found to have large numbers of CD8 lymphocytes that actively suppressed HIV reproduction. HIV-infected people with large numbers of CD8 cells were also less likely to transmit the infection to

Legacy of the Black Death

Where did the defective CCR5 gene come from? Stephen O'Brien, a genetics expert at the National Cancer Institute, has studied the gene in various people and calculated that the defective form that provides some protection against HIV first appeared about seven hundred years ago. In some places it is quite common, with one copy present in nearly 14 percent of the population and two copies present in one percent. Unusual genes do not usually get to be that common unless they give the people that have them some advantage in the struggle for survival—such as protection against a deadly disease. But AIDS did not exist seven hundred years ago. The big killer disease then was bubonic plague, the Black Death that wiped out a large fraction of the population of Europe in the fourteenth century. The defective CCR5 gene is most common now precisely among people whose ancestors came from the large plague areas of Europe. They are descendants of people who survived the Black Death in the Middle Ages. Could this gene have protected their ancestors from bubonic plague? Medical researchers have found that both HIV and the bacterium that causes plague attack macrophages. Stanley Falkow, a microbiologist at Stanford University, began studies in 1998 designed to find out whether the AIDS resistance gene stops the plague bacterium from infecting macrophages or if it protects against the disease by causing the white blood cells that are infected to kill themselves before the infection can spread.[23]

sex partners. These findings suggest that a vaccine that stimulates these killer T cells might be effective in preventing AIDS.[24]

The Rocky Road to an AIDS Vaccine

For many years, researchers have been trying to develop a vaccine to protect people against HIV. One reason progress has been slow is that the virus mutates so readily and rapidly. Vaccines against other diseases usually consist of a virus that has been killed (with heat or chemicals) or weakened so that it stimulates the formation of protective antibodies without itself causing disease. In some cases particular antigens from the surface of the virus are used to make vaccines. These portions, or subunits, of the virus are used either by themselves or combined with some tame vaccine virus such as vaccinia, the cowpox virus that was used for vaccination against smallpox. But the AIDS virus and its antigens are constantly changing, so a vaccine that is effective against the HIV strain current one day may be utterly helpless to protect against the strains that will be around a week later.

The efforts of researchers trying to make a successful subunit vaccine have been focused mainly on parts of HIV that are so essential to its survival that they are unlikely to change much over time. One of these is the gp120 protein. Although this protein is quite variable, researchers have found that part of it remains basically the same from one HIV form to another. There are limits to how much this part can change because it must be exactly the right shape to grab onto the receptors on helper T cells. Although some researchers have doubts about whether a vaccine based on gp120 can really protect people against HIV, in 1998 the FDA approved large-scale human tests of such a vaccine on 5,000 volunteers in the United States and 2,500 in

Thailand. This vaccine, produced by VaxGen (a division of the biotechnology company Genentech), is targeted against the gp120 proteins in two of the most common strains of HIV-1. In tests on chimpanzees, the vaccine protected the animals against very high doses of the virus, says Donald Francis, the chief researcher and president of VaxGen. "It works in a chimp, it's safe in humans, and it produces a better immune response in humans than in chimps," Dr. Francis stated. "To sit back and wait for more lab tests would, I think, be unconscionable."[25]

Various techniques may be used to make vaccines against HIV more effective. One subunit vaccine, for example, was

The NAMES Project AIDS Memorial Quilt, on display in Washington, D.C., in 1992, is in memory of those who have died from AIDS. Researchers hope to decrease the numbers of people who die from the disease by someday creating an HIV vaccine.

made by inserting the gene for an HIV outer protein (gp160) into live vaccinia virus. An injection of this vaccine, followed by a booster shot of a different subunit vaccine, for example, stimulated much stronger antibody responses than the first vaccine alone. It also stimulated the production of killer T cells specifically targeted to HIV.[26] Harvard researcher Ronald Desrosiers found in tests on monkeys that removing the sugars that normally cover the gp120 protein greatly increased the production of virus-neutralizing antibodies.[27]

Researchers at Genentech are working on a different approach. They have developed microspheres (tiny capsules made from a plasticlike substance that dissolves in the body) containing protein fragments from HIV-1, together with an immune stimulator, QS-21. The tiny microspheres are injected with an ordinary syringe and release their contents slowly, over about a month. In experiments on baboons, the combination stimulated much greater formation of effective anti-HIV antibodies than the proteins alone.[28] Chiron Corp. and the French drug company Rhone-Poulenc are combining a traditional vaccine (which stimulates the production of antibodies) with a vaccine using one of HIV's inner-core proteins to stimulate killer T cells. Researchers at Merck & Co., are trying another approach, producing a vaccine with "naked DNA"—HIV genes, instead of proteins or the whole virus.[29]

Some researchers believe that the best protection against AIDS would be provided by a live-virus vaccine, prepared from an attenuated (weakened) strain of HIV. This raises some serious questions, however. AIDS is so deadly that there must be no chance that the vaccine itself will cause it. But how can that be guaranteed when the virus mutates so readily? On whom could such a vaccine be tested? Much of the vaccine research so far has been done on chimpanzees and monkeys. In the United States, regulatory agencies have been reluctant to approve tests of a potentially dangerous vaccine on humans. The commercial companies producing

An Edible Vaccine?

Genetic engineers have been doing amazing things. They have spliced human genes into the chromosomes of cows so that valuable biochemicals can be obtained in large quantities from the cows' milk. They have introduced firefly genes into plants so that their leaves glow when they are exposed to oxygen. Now Dutch AIDS researcher Jaap Goudsmit is using genetic engineering in an effort to solve the problem of delivering an AIDS vaccine to people in developing countries that would be inexpensive, easily distributed, and readily accepted. He aims to make a painless vaccine that people can eat.

In collaboration with Charles Arntzen at Cornell University in Ithaca, New York, Goudsmit has already introduced HIV genes into potato plants, yielding potatoes that contain HIV proteins. Laboratory mice that ate the potatoes had increased immune defenses against HIV-1. The next step will be to use a plant food that is more familiar to people in Africa, Asia, and South America—bananas, for instance. A way will also have to be found to get people's immune systems to attack the virus proteins in the bananas without rejecting the whole banana. (Normally we can tolerate foreign proteins in foods—we would never be able to get nourishment from them otherwise.) Such an edible vaccine could be grown and administered by the local people themselves, rather than by outsiders, who may be mistrusted and feared.[30]

vaccines are worried about liability and the possibility of multimillion-dollar lawsuits if anything goes wrong. The average person, even in high-risk groups, finds the idea of taking anything with the name AIDS attached to it rather scary.[31]

In 1997 a group of fifty physicians and AIDS activists made headlines by volunteering to be injected with a live, attenuated HIV vaccine. Members of the Chicago-based International Association of Physicians in AIDS Care (IAPAC) proposed designing a live-vaccine trial, for which FDA approval would be sought. Meanwhile, however, researchers working with live SIV vaccines in monkeys and chimpanzees have reported that after the first apparent successes, some of the animals that had seemed to be protected later progressed to severe AIDS-like symptoms. Primate researcher Ronald Desrosiers cautions that an attenuated HIV vaccine should be offered only to people who are at high risk of becoming infected. In the first vaccine trials, he says, researchers should be super-cautious, and even then there may be some bad results. "Is it going to be absolutely, 100% safe? Forget it. It never will be. If you put it into enough people, there will be problems."[32]

Recent studies suggest that concerns about the safety of an attenuated vaccine may be quite realistic. At the Twelfth World AIDS Conference in Geneva in 1998, Ruth Ruprecht of the Dana Farber Cancer Institute in Boston reported the "rather sobering news" that an attenuated SIV vaccine tested on monkeys caused active development of AIDS in the some of the vaccinated animals. Despite this report, Los Angeles AIDS specialist Charles Farthing, the leader of the group of doctors who had volunteered to test a live vaccine, said that he was still willing to volunteer and would take the new drug combinations if anything went wrong.[33]

What About the World?

The spectacular advances researchers have been making toward effective treatments for AIDS have been great news—for those who can afford them. But what do they mean for the majority of people with AIDS throughout the world? Supplying the latest treatments to all who could benefit from them would strain the budgets of local and national governments in wealthy countries. For developing nations, which cannot afford even disposable lancets for blood tests, multi-thousand-dollar-a-year treatments for each AIDS patient or even vaccinations against HIV (if safe and effective vaccines can be developed) are simply out of the question. And yet, as Peter Piot, executive director of UNAIDS in Geneva, Switzerland, pointed out in a guest editorial in the journal *Science*, "Ignoring the AIDS research needs of 90% of the individuals affected by the epidemic is not only unethical, it is irrational, for a global pandemic such as AIDS can only be stopped if the problem is tackled on all fronts."[34]

How can the benefits of AIDS research be brought to the whole world? London-based syndicated columnist Gwynne Dyer has speculated on possibilities for the future of AIDS. Noting that drug companies normally charge prices for their few successful products that are far above their actual production costs in order to recoup their huge investments in research and development, he says that even an HIV vaccine would still be far out of reach of the average African. A course of vaccinations costing about $200 per person, for example, would mean a cost of $50 billion to $75 billion to protect most of the Africans who are at risk. Not to do so would "condemn Africa to a slow-motion holocaust of human lives that destroys families, sabotages development, and will ultimately leave it even poorer than before. But where would that kind of money come from?" One possibility is that drug companies might sell their products to Africans at cost; another is that the rich countries might chip in to pay for vaccines for Africa. Is either of these things likely to happen? Dyer advises, "Don't hold your breath." But, he speculates, South Africa might well decide to gain influence in Africa by defying patent laws and producing the needed drugs and vaccines at cost. The drug companies would be reluctant to sue them, he says, for fear of a public-relations disaster that could lead to tighter regulation of their drug-pricing policies.[35]

Meanwhile, in 1998 several drug companies announced that they were cutting their prices by 50 to 75 percent for AIDS drugs to be sold in developing countries in Africa, Asia, and South America. GlaxoWellcome, for example, would sell their combination of AZT and 3TC for $200 a month or less. It was doubtful, however, how big a dent these reductions could make in the worldwide AIDS epidemic. In Uganda, for example, an estimated 1.8 million people are infected with HIV. With the new price cuts, a triple drug combination would cost about $400 a month. But the average middle-class Ugandan earns only $500 a month. Health insurance is rare there, and the Ugandan government has refused to pay for the drugs. UNAIDS estimated that about three thousand people would be able to afford the drugs at the reduced prices.[36]

AIDS and the Internet

The efforts to make up-to-date AIDS information available to anyone who needs it, anywhere in the world, have been greatly aided by the explosive growth of the Internet. Postings on the World Wide Web and various newsgroups provide information for people at every level, from schoolchildren up to medical specialists. Normally when a major scientific conference is held, a flurry of scattered news

Success Story: Education Works

In 1991, when most nations in Asia were still insisting that they did not have an AIDS problem, the leaders of Thailand faced some hard realities. Population experts estimated that if nothing was done, this small Asian nation would have between 2 million and 4 million people infected with HIV by the year 2000, and AIDS deaths would rise so rapidly that the average Thai life expectancy would drop from seventy-five to forty-five by the year 2010. That is not happening, however. The government turned to Mechai Viravaidya, the director of the Population and Community Development Association, who had earned the nickname of the Condom King by organizing a highly successful voluntary birth control program in the 1970s. In 1991, at the request of the Thai government, Mechai set up a massive public education program. Television and radio stations were required to broadcast half a minute of AIDS education every hour. AIDS education programs were set up in the last two years of primary schools, as well as in offices and factories and in rural communities. Movie and television companies received government subsidies for including AIDS themes in films and soap operas. Instead of continuing to rise, new AIDS cases hit their peak in 1991 and then started to fall. There was a 77 percent decline in other sexually transmitted diseases as well. "The projections for the year 2000 are no longer relevant," says Mechai. "Behavior change has occurred."[37]

reports hit the highlights, and the text of the reports is published in a journal or book many months later. During the historic 1996 AIDS conference in Vancouver, however, the highlights of each day's reports were posted on a special Web site the next day, for anyone with Internet access to read.[38] Other sites provide solutions to specific problems. (Caution is needed in consulting such sites, however, since anyone can post information and not all of it is accurate.)

Researcher David Ho has commented on how the Internet has revolutionized research: "The ability to collaborate through email has been critical. And not just text—we attach spreadsheets and graphics with test results. My closest collaborator is a biomathematician at Los Alamos National Laboratory 2,000 miles away. As soon as we're done running an assay here, he has the results. What we can do in a few hours used to take three weeks. I'd say this sort of technology has moved our progress tenfold."[39]

In 1996, a twenty-four-hour-a-day global electronic conference called Program for Collaboration Against AIDS and Related Epidemics (ProCAARE) was set up by Satellife Inc., a nonprofit organization based in Boston. Shortly after Procaare started posting information, a doctor in Pakistan asked for advice on HIV home care services. "A day later," says Dr. Richard Marlink, executive director of the Harvard AIDS Institute and a codirector of ProCAARE, "he got a response from Puerto Rico with a report on their home-care project. And the next day he received a similar response from Zambia. All this occurred without the industrialized countries." In the developing countries, mail service is very slow, and a phone call between Pakistan and Zambia costs twenty dollars a minute; the ability to share information by electronic mail can bring major benefits to medical practitioners.[40] Some internet addresses for AIDS information are listed on pp. 156–157.

Laypersons, too—both young and old—can research

medical topics on the Web and share their experiences and concerns. One notable Web site is maintained by HOT, the Healthy Oakland Teens Project. Aimed at reducing adolescents' risk for HIV infection, HOT uses peer role models to advocate for responsible decision making, healthy values, and communication skills. The Web site, <http://www. caps.ucsf.edu/capsweb/hotindex.html>, offers photos and stories about the HOT project at an urban, ethnically diverse junior high school in Oakland, California. It also provides a complete curriculum for a health education unit on AIDS, including background information and thought-provoking discussion questions.

From scientists on the front lines of AIDS research to doctors coping with the day-to-day problems of treating patients and to ordinary people trying to understand the HIV epidemic and what it means to them—all have a part in fighting AIDS. New technological tools, such as the Internet, which has linked the world into a global community, are helping in the battle to control this deadly disease.

Q & A

Q. *My friend is HIV positive. Can I catch AIDS by using the same towel he used?*

A. No. HIV does not survive for long in contact with air and is not transmitted by casual contact. But you might pick it up if you share your friend's razor and both of you cut yourselves, or from a shared toothbrush if you both have bleeding gums.

Q. *I heard you can catch AIDS by "sexual contact." Does that include kissing?*

A. Theoretically yes, but it's not very likely. A friendly kiss is safe, but a long, deep, open-mouthed kiss could possibly transmit the AIDS virus if both people have mouth sores or bleeding gums.

Q. *My boyfriend has had sexual experiences with other people, but he is clean and healthy and says he is HIV negative. Do we need to use condoms?*

A. Yes. Even if you trust your boyfriend to tell the truth, he may be infected without knowing it. If he has had a negative test, it may have been taken too soon after infection for antibodies to show up. And looking healthy is no guarantee—people infected with HIV are most likely to transmit the virus in the early stages of the infection, before any symptoms have appeared.

Q. *Some kids at camp were HIV positive, and I was in the swimming pool with them. Do I need to get an AIDS test?*

A. No. Even if they had a bleeding cut, the water in the pool would have diluted the virus, so no one would have taken in enough to become infected. Also, the chlorine in the pool kills HIV.

Q. *Can you catch AIDS if you have sex just once?*

A. Yes. Your chances of becoming infected with HIV increase with the number of sex partners and acts of intercourse, but people have become infected in a single sexual encounter.

Q. *Can you catch AIDS from a mosquito bite?*

A. Some scientists believe this is theoretically possible, but it is not very likely. The germs that cause diseases transmitted by mosquitoes or flies generally are able to multiply inside the insect's body; HIV does not do this. In tropical Africa, where both insect-transmitted diseases and AIDS are now very common, AIDS still occurs mainly in sexually active adults and in children of HIV-infected mothers; insect-transmitted diseases strike young and old alike, and HIV does not.

Q. *My boyfriend says we don't need to use condoms because he never had sex with anybody else. Is that right?*

A. What people say when they want to have sex is not always the truth. And when you have sex with someone, you may be exposing yourself to all the sexually transmitted diseases carried by anyone else he or she had sex with in his or her entire life. Abstain or use a condom.

Q. *Is it safe to have sex as long as we use a condom?*

A. The only completely "safe sex" is abstinence. Latex condoms used with a water-based lubricant containing a spermicide such as nonoxynol-9 usually provide good protection against transmitting HIV, but they may leak or break.

Q. *I just found out that someone I had sex with is HIV positive. Should I get tested for AIDS?*

A. Yes. And if the test is negative, it should be repeated six months later to make sure.

Q. *I tried to give blood, but they said my blood tested HIV positive. What should I do?*

A. First, don't panic. Talk to an AIDS counselor and get as much information as you can. Have the test repeated and confirmed before you consider any treatments. Consult a doctor who has experience in treating people with AIDS. Whether to start treatments right away is your personal decision, but experts say prompt treatment may keep you healthy.

AIDS Chronology

1969—Robert R. dies of AIDS (confirmed by tests in 1986) in St. Louis.

1981—First reports of unusual immune system failure in United States gay men; Gay Men's Health Crisis (first AIDS organization) founded.

1982—The new disease, also found in hemophiliacs, is named AIDS.

1983—AIDS reported in two women who caught it from sex partners; people at high risk of AIDS asked not to donate blood; Luc Montagnier reports finding a virus linked to AIDS.

1984—Robert Gallo announces isolation of AIDS virus.

1985—First HIV antibody test approved in United States; first story about Ryan White; Rock Hudson dies of AIDS.

1986—AIDS virus is named HIV (human immunodeficiency virus).

1987—FDA approves AZT (first anti-AIDS drug) for experimental use; AIDS Memorial Quilt is started.

1988—First World AIDS Day.

1990—Ryan White dies; Congress passes funding legislation in his name; FDA approves first test kit for HIV-2.

1991—Magic Johnson announces he is HIV positive; FDA approves ddI.

1992—Gallo and Montagnier agree that they both worked with the same virus, which came from Montagnier's lab; Congress bans the use of federal funds for needle-exchange programs.

1993—CDC expands case definition of AIDS; FDA approves female condom; U.S. Postal Service issues twenty-nine-cent stamp with AIDS red ribbon symbol.

1994—NIH announces that AZT treatment lowers the risk of HIV transfer from mother to infant; United Nations forms UNAIDS program.

1995—Researchers find that HIV reproduces rapidly beginning right from first infection; first National HIV Testing Day; FDA approves first protease inhibitor.

1996—Additional receptors for HIV are found on T lymphocytes; FDA approves first HIV home test kit, HIV RNA test, and saliva-based test kit; mutant CCR5 gene for resistance to HIV is found; three-drug cocktail is reported to be effective treatment; researcher David Ho is named *Time* magazine's Man of the Year.

1997—First enthusiasm for drug cocktails fades, but statistics show that in the United States, AIDS death rate and number of new cases dropped for the first time in 1996, and the downward trends continue; FDA approves the first drug combination pill, Combivir (AZT + 3TC).

1998—The United Nations reports that more than 30 million people in the world are HIV infected, and the epidemic is spreading rapidly in developing nations; researchers work out the complete three-dimensional structure of the part of HIV that attaches to CD4 cells and take pictures of how the virus attacks a cell; FDA approves large-scale human trials of a vaccine against HIV.

For More Information

ACT UP (AIDS Coalition to Unleash Power)
135 West 29 Street, 10th Floor
New York, NY 10001
Hot line: (212) 564-2437

AIDS Clinical Trials Information Service
P.O. Box 6421
Rockville, MD 20849
(800) TRIALS-A [(800) 874-2572]

AIDS Project Los Angeles
1313 N. Vine Street
Los Angeles, CA 90028
(213) 993-1600
Hot line: (800) 922-AIDS

Centers for Disease Control and Prevention
National AIDS Hot line
(800) 342-2437

Gay Men's Health Crisis
129 West 20 Street
New York, NY 10011
(212) 807-6664

National Association of People with AIDS
1413 K Street, NW, 7th Floor
Washington, DC 20005
(202) 848-0414

National Minority AIDS Council
1931 Thirteenth Street, NW
Washington, DC 20009
(202) 483-6622

Project Inform
1965 Market Street, Suite 220
San Francisco, CA 94103
(800) 822-7422

The NAMES Project Foundation
310 Townsend Street, Suite 310
San Francisco, CA 94107
(415) 882-5500

Women's Information Service and Exchange (WISE)
125 Fifth Street, NE
Atlanta, GA 30308
(800) 326-3861

Chapter Notes

Chapter 1. A New Plague

1. John Gallagher, "Johnson Disclosure Brings AIDS Issues to Middle America," *The Advocate*, December 17, 1991, p. 14.

2. Pico Iyer, "It Can Happen to Anybody. Even Magic Johnson," *Time*, November 18, 1991, p. 26.

3. Elizabeth Neus, "Magic Learns of Fear and Loathing," *The Courier-News* (Bridgewater, N.J.), November 5, 1992, p. A7; Michael Martinez, "Citing 'Controversies,' Johnson Retires Again," *The New York Times*, November 3, 1992, p. B9.

4. The Associated Press, "Players Happy Magic's Back," *The Courier-News* (Bridgewater, N.J.), January 30, 1996, pp. C1, C3.

5. Lorrie Lynch, "Who's News?" *USA Weekend*, May 29–31, 1998, p. 2.

6. Magic Johnson, "I'm Not Going to Stop Being Me," *Los Angeles Times*, November 3, 1996, <http://www.latimes.com/HOME/NEWS/SPORTS/REPORTS/AIDS/magic.htm> (October 9, 1998).

7. CDC, "International Projections/Statistics," *Technical Information Activity*, January 27, 1998, <http://www.cdc.gov/nchstp/hiv_aids/stats/internat.htm> (October 9, 1998).

8. CDC, *HIV/AIDS Surveillance Report*, Year-end edition, vol. 9, no. 2, June 23, 1998, p. 19.

9. Kim Painter, "AIDS Deaths Drop 26%, Lifting Hope," *The Courier-News* (Bridgewater, N.J.), September 12, 1997, p. A1.

10. CDC, *HIV/AIDS Surveillance Report*, p. 16.

11. Mark Schoofs, "AIDS Ed in the 'Hood," *The Body: An AIDS and HIV Information Resource*, May 19, 1998, <http://www.thebody.com/schoofs/hood.html> (October 9, 1998).

Chapter 2. The History of AIDS

1. Randy Shilts, *And the Band Played On* (New York: Quality Paperback Book Club, 1993), pp. 42–43, 48–49, 55–56, 61–63.

2. Ibid., pp. 66–68; "Pneumocystis Pneumonia—Los Angeles," *Morbidity and Mortality Weekly Report*, June 5, 1981, pp. 250–252.

3. Shilts, pp. 68–77, 80–81; "Kaposi's Sarcoma and Pneumocystis Pneumonia Among Homosexual Men—New York City and California," *Morbidity and Mortality Weekly Report*, July 3 1981, pp. 305–308.

4. Steven Epstein, *Impure Science* (Berkeley: University of California Press, 1996), pp. 45–56.

5. Shilts, pp. 130–131, 137–138, 147, 200.

6. Epstein, pp. 66–77; Peter Radetsky, *The Invisible Invaders* (Boston: Little, Brown, and Co., 1991), pp. 323–329.

7. Radetsky, p. 332.

8. Ibid., pp. 333–339.

9. Philip J. Hilts, "Challenge Arises to a New Claim by U.S. AIDS Researcher," *The New York Times*, March 13, 1991, p. A23; Jon Cohen, "HHS: Gallo Guilty of Misconduct," *Science*, January 8, 1993, pp. 168–170; Christopher Anderson, "ORI Drops Gallo Case in Legal Dispute," *Science*, November 19, 1993, pp. 1202–1204.

10. Associated Press, "French Scientists to Receive Royalties from AIDS Test Kit," *The Courier-News* (Bridgewater, N.J.), July 12, 1994, p. A5.

11. Philip J. Hilts, "Key Patent on AIDS to Favor the French," *The New York Times*, July 12, 1994, p. C10.

12. K. A. Fackelmann, "Accord Ends Feud over AIDS Blood Test," *Science News*, July 16, 1994, p. 37.

13. Lawrence K. Altman, "H.I.V. Is Linked to a Subspecies of Chimpanzee," *The New York Times*, February 1, 1999, p. A1.

14. Marc Lapp, *Evolutionary Medicine* (San Francisco: Sierra Club Books, 1994), p. 115; Ibid., pp. 86–92.

Chapter 3. What Is AIDS?

1. Michael Thomas Ford, *100 Questions & Answers About AIDS* (New York: Beech Tree, 1993), pp. 42–53.

2. Beth Sherman, "AIDS Drains Those Nursing the Victims," *The Courier-News* (Bridgewater, N.J.), June 6, 1993, p. B-10.

3. Gerald J. Stine, *AIDS Update 1998* (Upper Saddle River, N.J.: Prentice Hall, 1998), p. 31; CDC, "Revision of the Surveillance Case Definition of Acquired Immunodeficiency Syndrome," *Morbidity and Mortality Weekly Report*, vol. 36, 1987, pp. 3S–15S.

4. Steven Epstein, *Impure Science* (Berkeley: University of California Press, 1996), p. 288.

5. CDC, "1993 Revised Classification System for HIV Infection and Expanded Surveillance Case Definition for AIDS among Adolescents and Adults," *Morbidity and Mortality Weekly Report*, vol. 41, 1992, pp. 1–19.

6. Stine, p. 33; Lawrence K. Altman, "AIDS Cases Increase among Heterosexuals," *The New York Times*, March 11, 1994, p. A12.

7. Roberta J. Wong, "Overview of HIV Infection," *Pharmacy Times*, November 1994, p. 79.

8. CDC, *HIV/AIDS Surveillance Report*, vol. 9, no. 2, 1998, p. 10.

9. Ibid., pp. 11–13, 15.

10. CDC, "Young People at Risk—Epidemic Shifts Further Toward Young Women and Minorities," *Geneva 98 Background*, July 1998, <http://www.cdcnac.org/geneva98/issues/fyouth1.htm> (October 9, 1998).

11. UNAIDS and WHO, *Report on the Global HIV/AIDS Epidemic*, June 1998, pp. 6, 10, 11, 13, 14.

12. Peter Radetsky, *The Invisible Invaders* (Boston: Little, Brown, and Co., 1991), p. 340.

13. David Ho, "Pathogenesis of HIV Infection," *International AIDS Society—USA*, vol. 3, 1995, pp. 9–12.

14. Eve Lackritz et al, "Estimated Risk of Transmission of Human Immonodeficiency Virus by Screened Blood in the United States," *New England Journal of Medicine*, vol. 333, 1995, pp. 1721–1725.

15. CDC, *HIV/AIDS Surveillance Report*, p. 10.

16. Lawrence K. Altman, "AIDS Link to V.D. Becomes Clearer," *The New York Times*, June 11, 1993, p. A6; AP, "Study Indicates Why Herpes Is Factor in the Spread of AIDS," *The New York Times*, January 24, 1997, p. A14.

17. Norman Hearst and Stephen B. Hulley, "Preventing the Heterosexual Spread of AIDS: Are We Giving Our Patients the Best Advice?" *Journal of the American Medical Association*, vol. 259, 1988, p. 2428.

18. Stine, pp. 229–230, 332.

19. Lawrence K. Altman, "Nonvirulent H.I.V. Strain Found in Infected Group," *The New York Times*, October 9, 1992, p. A19; "Docs Say Genetic Defect Wards Off AIDS Infection," *Star Ledger* (Newark, N.J.), August 9, 1996; Greg Folkers, "Mutant Gene Not Sole Explanation for HIV Non-Progression," *NIAID News*, September 15, 1997, <http://www.niaid.nih.gov/newsroom/nonprogress.htm> (October 9, 1998).

20. Elizabeth Pennisi, "Microglial Madness," *Science News*, December 4, 1993, pp. 378–379; Herbert B. Newton, "Common Neurologic Complications of HIV-1 Infection and AIDS," *American Family Physician*, February 1, 1995, pp. 387–398.

Chapter 4. Diagnosing AIDS

1. Dan Chu, "A Boy Who Died in 1969 May Have Been America's First AIDS Victim," *People*, November 16, 1987, pp. 179–180; Christine Gorman, "Strange Trip Back to the Future," *Time*, November 9, 1987, p. 83; Gina Kolata, "Boy's 1969 Death Suggests AIDS Invaded U.S. Several Times," *The New York Times*, October 28, 1987, p. A15.

2. Michael Thomas Ford, *101 Questions & Answers About AIDS* (New York: Beach Tree Books, 1992), pp. 110–113.

3. Gerald J. Stine, *AIDS Update 1998* (Upper Saddle River, N.J.: Prentice Hall, 1998), pp. 344–361; Grace Brooke Huffman, "Accuracy of HIV Testing with an Oral Mucosal Swab," *American Family Physician*, May 15, 1997, pp. 2517–2518.

4. Stine, pp. 362–363; Lawrence K. Altman, "New Test for Progression to AIDS," *The New York Times*, June 4, 1996, p. C3; S. Sternberg, "New Tests Mark Big Leap in HIV Diagnosis," *Science News*, July 20, 1996, p. 36.

5. Stine, p. 349.

6. J. Raloff, "Targeting Hospital Screening for HIV," *Science News*, August 15, 1992, p. 103; AP, "Maryland Officials Are Accused of Forcing Man to Test for H.I.V.," *The New York Times*, March 13, 1994, p. 20; Gabriel Rotello, "AIDS Is Still an Exceptional Disease," *The New York Times*, August 22, 1997, p. A23.

7. "Agreement Reached over AIDS Assistance," *The Courier-News* (Bridgewater, N.J.), May 2, 1996; AP, "AMA Backing Testing for HIV," *The Courier-News* (Bridgewater, N.J.), June 28, 1996, p. A3.

8. Ralph Siegel, "Rape Victims Can Order AIDS Test for Attacker," *The Courier-News* (Bridgewater, N.J.), September 26, 1997, p. A1.

9. Stine, pp. 363–366; Karyn Snyder, "In Confidence: FDA Approves Home Care Kit to Test for HIV Virus," *Drug Topics*, June 10, 1996, pp. 120–122.

10. Daniel Q. Haney, "Most HIV-Positive Know Status," *The Courier-News* (Bridgewater, N.J.), September 29, 1997, p. A3.

Chapter 5. Treating AIDS

1. Michael Waldholz, "New Drug 'Cocktails' Mark Exciting Turn In the War on AIDS," *The Wall Street Journal*, June 14, 1996, p. A1.

2. Ibid., p. A6.

3. Michael Waldholz, "AIDS Conferees Debate How Early to Offer New Drugs," *The Wall Street Journal*, July 12, 1996, p. B1.

4. John G. Bartlett and Richard D. Moore, "Improving HIV Therapy," *Scientific American*, July 1998, p. 92.

5. John Leland, "The End of AIDS?" *Newsweek*, December 2, 1996, pp. 64–68; Katie Rodgers, "New Hope: Viramune Approved for Treatment of AIDS," *Drug Topics*, July 2, 1996, p. 33.

6. Leland, pp. 67, 69; Gerald J. Stine, *AIDS Update 1998* (Upper Saddle River, N.J.: Prentice Hall, 1998), pp. 68–72.

7. Bartlett and Moore, p. 87.

8. Michael Waldholz, "New Drug 'Cocktails' Mark Exciting Turn in the War on AIDS," p. A6; Elizabeth K. Wilson, "AIDS Conference Highlights Hope of Drug Cocktails, Chemokine Research," *Chemical & Engineering News*, July 29, 1996, pp. 42–45; Jon Cohen, "Stubborn HIV Reservoirs Vulnerable to New Treatments," *Science*, May 9, 1997, pp. 898–899.

9. Philip Elmer-DeWitt, "Turning the Tide," *Time*, December 30, 1996, pp. 54–55; Christine Gorman, "The Disease Detective," *Time*, December 30, 1996, pp. 56–64; Howard Chua-Eoan, "The Tao of Ho," *Time*, December 30, 1996, pp. 69–70.

10. Jon Cohen, "HIV Suppressed Long After Treatment," *Science*, September 26, 1997, p. 1927.

11. Michael Waldholz, "Some AIDS Cases Defy New Drug 'Cocktails,' but Success in Many Others Is Cutting Hospital Costs," *The Wall Street Journal*, October 10, 1996, pp. B1, B7; Lawrence K. Altman, "With AIDS Advance, More Disappointment," *The New York Times*, January 19, 1997, pp. 1, 14; Sheryl Gay Stolberg, "Despite New AIDS Drugs, Many Still Lose the Battle," *The New York Times*, August 22, 1997, pp. A1, A20; AP, "F.D.A. Warns of Diabetes Risk in AIDS Drugs," *The New York Times*, June 12, 1997, p. A22; Daniel J. Haney, "AIDS Drugs Lose Luster," *The New York Times*, September 30, 1997, p. A1.

12. Bartlett and Moore, p. 91; Denise Grady, "Study Says H.I.V. Tests Underestimate Women's Risk," *The New York Times*, November 6, 1998, p. A18.

13. Elizabeth Neus, "AIDS Guidelines Urge Trio of Drugs," *The Courier-News* (Bridgewater, N.J.), June 20, 1997, p. A3.

14. Michael Shernoff, "A History of Hope: The HIV Roller Coaster," *FOCUS: A Guide to AIDS Research and Counseling*, June 1997, <http://members.aol.com/therapysvc/hope.htm> (October 9, 1998).

15. Michael Waldholz, "New AIDS Treatment Raises Tough Question of Who Will Get It," *The Wall Street Journal*, July 3, 1996, pp. A1, A12; Jean McCann, "The AIDS Front: Are Cures and Compliance Within Reach for Patients?" *Drug Topics*, February 17, 1997, pp. 60–62, 65–66, 68; Deborah Sontag and Lynda Richardson, "Doctors Withhold H.I.V. Pill Regimen from Some," *The New York Times*, March 2, 1997, pp. 1, 35.

16. *Los Angeles Times*, "Selectivity in Treating AIDS Worries Some," *The Courier-News* (Bridgewater, N.J.), August 24, 1997, p. A9.

17. "U.S. Unit Says FDA Clears Combivir Tablet for AIDS," *The Wall Street Journal*, September 30, 1997, p. B6; Ed Sussman, "AZT Not Needed in AIDS Cocktails," *United Press International*, September 29, 1997; provided by the CDC National AIDS Clearinghouse, © 1997, Information, Inc., Bethesda, Md.

18. Associated Press, "F.D.A. Approves an AIDS Drug That Is Taken Just Once a Day," *The New York Times*, September 19, 1998, p. A7; "Sustiva Approved in U.S. As Part of HIV Combination Therapy," *Doctor's Guide*, September 18, 1998, <http:www.pslgroup.com/dg/affde.htm> (October 9, 1998).

19. Christine Gorman, "What, I'm Gonna Live?" *Time*, October 14, 1996, pp. 77–78.

20. "Hype, Hope and Hurt on the AIDS Front Lines," *The New York Times*, February 2, 1997, p. E3.

21. Mireya Navarro, "Growing Up in the Shadow of the AIDS Virus," *The New York Times*, March 21, 1993, pp. 33, 36.

Chapter 6. Preventing AIDS

1. Lynn Minton, "Fresh Voices," *Parade Magazine*, December 27, 1992, p. 12.

2. Kate Shindle, *Preventing HIV Transmission in America*, pamphlet from the Miss America Organization, 1998.

3. "NYC School Board OKs Instruction about AIDS for Young Schoolkids," *The Courier-News* (Bridgewater, N.J.), June 26, 1992, p. A5.

4. James Dao, "Critics Decry New AIDS Education Rules as Censorship," *The New York Times*, May 29, 1992, p. B3.

5. Thomas J. Coates and Chris Collins, "Preventing HIV Infection," *Scientific American*, July 1998, p. 97.

6. Mark Schoofs, "AIDS Ed in the 'Hood," *The Body: An AIDS and HIV Information Resource*, May 19, 1998, <http://www.thebody.com/schoofs/hood.html> (October 9, 1998); Michael Thomas Ford, *100 Questions & Answers about AIDS* (New York: Beech Tree Books, 1993), pp. 100–103.

7. John B. Jemmott III, Loretta Sweet Jemmott, and Geoffrey T. Fong, "Abstinence and Safer Sex HIV Risk-Reduction for African American Adolescents," *Journal of the American Medical Association*, vol. 279, May 20, 1998, pp. 1529–1536.

8. UNAIDS Review, "Sexual Health Education Does Lead to Safer Sexual Behavior," October 22, 1997, <http://www.us.unaids.org/highband/press/sexualhealth.html> (October 9, 1998).

9. Erik Strommen, "Rebuts View That Condoms Don't Protect Against HIV," *The Courier-News* (Bridgewater, N.J.), February 9, 1993, p. A9.

10. Heather Morrison, "Play It Safe—Not Just on AIDS Day," *The Courier-News* (Bridgewater, N.J.), November 30, 1994, p. A13.

11. Gerald J. Stine. *AIDS Update 1998* (Upper Saddle River, N.J.: Prentice-Hall, 1998), pp. 255–257.

12. Emory Thomas, Jr., "AZT Found to Sharply Reduce Passage of AIDS from Mothers to Their Infants," *The Wall Street Journal*, February 22, 1994, p. B2.

13. Stine, p. 302.

14. Lawrence K. Altman, "Drug Seems to Cut AIDS Infection for Workers Stuck with Needles," *The New York Times*, December 22, 1995, p. A32.

15. Mireya Navarro, "New York Needle Exchanges Called Surprisingly Effective," *The New York Times*, February 18, 1993, p. 1.

16. Elizabeth Neus, "Needle Exchange Programs Get Push," *The Courier-News* (Bridgewater, N.J.), December 10, 1995, p. A6.

17. CDC, "Syringe Exchange Programs—United States, 1994–1995," *Morbidity and Mortality Weekly Report*, September 22, 1995, p. 685.

18. "Pro & Con: Free Needles for Addicts, to Help Curb AIDS," *The New York Times*, December 20, 1987, p. E20.

19. Ronald Sullivan, "Yolanda Serrano, 45, Organizer of Anti-AIDS Needle Exchanges," *The New York Times*, October 22, 1993, p. B9.

20. Mireya Navarro, "New York City Resurrects Plan on NeedleSwap," *The New York Times*, January 14, 1992, p. A1.

21. "The Case for Clean Needles," *The New York Times,* October 11, 1993, p. A16.

22. Stine, p. 263.

23. Ibid., p. 265.

24. Associated Press, "Founders of Syringe Program Get Fines," *The Courier-News* (Bridgewater, N.J.), August 12, 1997, p. A2.

25. Mireya Navarro, "Addicts Use a Change in Law to Buy Needles at Pharmacies," *The New York Times,* March 7, 1993, p. 43; Stine, p. 265.

26. Lincoln E. Moses, "Needle Exchanges Do Limit HIV Transmission," *The Courier-News* (Bridgewater, N.J.), November 18, 1995, p. A13.

Chapter 7. AIDS and Society

1. "Breaking the Silence," *People*, March 6, 1995, pp. 64–74; "Louganis: I have AIDS," *The Courier-News* (Bridgewater, N.J.), February 23, 1995, p. C5.

2. Meg Grant, "An Anguished Voice Falls Silent," *People*, December 23, 1991, p. 114.

3. Ann Japenga, "The Secret," *Health*, September 1992, p. 44.

4. Norman Daniels, "HIV-Infected Professionals, Patient Rights, and the 'Switching Dilemma'," *Journal of the American Medical Association*, vol. 267, March 11, 1992, pp. 1368–1371.

5. Gerald J. Stine, *1998 AIDS Update* (Upper Saddle River, N.J.: Prentice-Hall, 1998), p. 302.

6. Joseph F. Sullivan, "New Jersey Judge Rules Surgeon With AIDS Must Tell Patients," *The New York Times*, April 26, 1991, p. B1.

7. "Bergalis Chronology," *The Courier-News* (Bridgewater, N.J.), December 9, 1991, p. A4.

8. "Panel Supports Doctors with HIV," *The Courier-News* (Bridgewater, N.J.), July 31, 1992, p. A3.

9. "Workers Can Keep AIDS Secret," *The Courier-News* (Bridgewater, N.J.), August 20, 1994, p. A2.

10. Mireya Navarro, "Diversity but Conflict Under Wider AIDS Umbrella," *The New York Times*, May 28, 1993, p. B1.

11. "Condom Campaign Launched on TV," *The Courier-News* (Bridgewater, N.J.), January 5, 1994, p. A1.

12. Stine, p. 390.

13. DeWayne Wickham, "Helms' Drive to Punish AIDS Victims Irrational," *The Courier-News* (Bridgewater, N.J.), July 8, 1995, p. A5.

14. Tom Ehrenfeld, "AIDS 'Heroes' and 'Villains,'" *Newsweek*, October 14, 1991, p. 10.

15. Al Kamen, "Court Bans AIDS Jobs Bias," *The Courier-News* (Bridgewater, N.J.), March 4, 1987, p. A3.

16. Linda Greenhouse, "Justices, 6-3, Bar Veto of Line Items in Bills; See H.I.V. as Disability," *The New York Times*, June 26, 1998, pp. A1, A18.

17. Gina Kolata, "AIDS Groups Dismayed by Report They See as Discounting Concern," *The New York Times*, February 7, 1993, p. 30.

18. Wickham, p. A5; Charles E. Cohen and Giovanna Breu, "A Year after Ryan White's Death, His Mother, Jeanne, Picks up the Pieces and Carries on His Fight," *People*, April 8, 1991, p. 118.

19. Stine, pp. 297, 299.

20. Eric Schmitt, "Bills Would Repeal Provision to Expel Troops with H.I.V.," *The New York Times*, January 27, 1996, p.A11.

21. Stine, pp. 297, 299.

22. Philip Shenon, "Threat Seen to Military's AIDS Research," *The New York Times*, February 2, 1996, p. 7.

23. "Failure to Tell of HIV Leads to Conviction," *Medical Tribune*, December 24, 1993, p. 7; "Possession of a Dangerous Weapon," *Time*, December 14, 1992, p. 23; Scott R. Akin, "States Crack Down on HIV Transmission," *The Advocate*, January 26, 1993, p. 22.

24. Robert Rudolph, "Sex Partner Held Liable for Concealing AIDS," *Star-Ledger* (Newark, N.J.), November 4, 1993, p. 21.

25. Joseph F. Sullivan, "Inmate with HIV Who Bit Guard Loses Appeal," *The New York Times*, February 18, 1993, p. B7.

26. "Man Infects Woman with HIV with Kiss," *The Courier-News* (Bridgewater, N.J.), July 11, 1997, p. A8.

27. Steven Epstein, *Impure Science* (Berkeley: University of California Press, 1996), pp. 216–217.

28. Ibid., p. 217.

29. Ibid., p. 219.

30. "Ritonavir and Indinavir: New Protease Inhibitors for AIDS," *Medical Sciences Bulletin*, April 1996, p. 1.

31. Elizabeth Neus, "Activists Push FDA to OK Drugs Faster," *The Courier-News* (Bridgewater, N.J.), July 16, 1995, p. A9.

32. Anthony Turney, The NAMES Project Foundation (postcard), October 9–11, 1992; "The AIDS Memorial Quilt," 1997, <http://www.aidsquilt.org> (October 9, 1998).

33. Lynn Minton, "Fresh Voices," *Parade Magazine*, December 27, 1992, p. 12.

Chapter 8. The Future of AIDS

1. Michael Waldholz, "New Drug 'Cocktails' Mark Exciting Turn In the War on AIDS," *The Wall Street Journal*, June 14, 1996, p. A6.

2. Daniel Q. Haney, Associated Press, "AIDS Drugs Lose Luster," *The Courier-News* (Bridgewater, N.J.), September 30, 1997, p. A1.

3. Lawrence K. Altman, "Immune System Can Revive After AIDS, Studies Suggest," *The New York Times*, July 2, 1998, p. A14.

4. Michael Waldholz, "Scientists Hope to Fix AIDS-Damaged Immune Systems," *The Wall Street Journal*, July 6, 1998, p. A18.

5. Elizabeth K. Wilson, "AIDS Conference Highlights Hope of Drug Cocktails, Chemokine Research," *Chemical & Engineering News*, July 29, 1996, pp. 42–46.

6. John Carey, "Locking HIV Out of White Blood Cells," *Business Week*, October 13, 1997, p. 126.

7. Nicholas Wade, "Scientists Take First Snapshots of AIDS Virus Attacking Cell," *The New York Times*, June 18, 1998, pp. A1, A33; "First Contact: Scientists Determine Structure of HIV-1 Protein that Grasps Human Cells," *HHMI News*, June 17, 1998, <http://www.hhmi.org/news/hendrickson.htm> (October 9, 1998); Michael Balter, "Revealing HIV's T Cell Passkey," *Science*, June 19, 1998, pp. 1833–1834.

8. Laurie K. Doepel, "'Trojan Horse' Virus Controls HIV Infection," *NIAID News*, September 4, 1997, <http://www. niaid.nih.gov/newsroom/VSV.htm> (October 9, 1998); Nicholas Wade, "Cattle Virus Is Redesigned to Attack H.I.V.," *The New York Times*, September 5, 1997, p. A32.

9. Jon Cohen, "How Can HIV Replication Be Controlled?" *Science*, May 28, 1993, p. 1257; Bree Scott-Hartland, "Common Alternative Therapies: Hypericin," *GMHC Treatment Issues*, Winter 1993/94, <http://www.aegis.com/pubs/gmhc/1993/ gm071117.html> (October 9, 1998); Martin A. Majchrowicz, "Hypericin," *Treatment Education Program*, Spring 1994, <http://www. primenet.com/~camilla/apla.hyp> (October 9, 1998).

10. Luis G. Santiago, "The Hydroxyurea Steamroller," *GMHC Treatment Issues*, November 1997, pp. 5–8.

11. David Weitzman, "HIV Team Corners Stealthy Enzyme," *New Scientist*, January 7, 1995, p. 13.

12. Wilson, pp. 42–46.

13. Gina Kolata, "Genetic Attacks on AIDS Readied," *The New York Times*, May 31, 1994, p. C1; Wilson da Silva, "Armed Cells Launch Twin Attack on AIDS," *New Scientist*, August 16, 1997, p. 10.

14. Kolata, p. C1; Lingxun Duan and Roger J. Pomerantz, "Intracellular Antibodies for HIV-1 Gene Therapy," *Science and Medicine*, May/June 1996, pp. 27–29.

15. Trisha Gura, "Antisense Has Growing Pains," *Science*, October 27, 1995, pp. 575–577; "Antisensical," *The Economist*, December 14, 1996, pp. 81–82.

16. John Carey, "A Tool for Staying a Step Ahead of HIV," *Business Week*, June 29, 1998, p. 89.

17. Michael Waldholz, "Drug May Lift T-Cells, a Key in AIDS Battle," *The Wall Street Journal*, October 31, 1996, pp. B1, B12; Mary Jean Pramik, "Interleukin-2 Shows Promise in Fighting Cancers, AIDS," *Hospital Pharmacist Report*, August 1997, p. 14.

18. Lawrence K. Altman, "Cross-Species Transplants Raise Concerns About Human Safety," *The New York Times*, January 9, 1996, pp. 11, 17; Lawrence K. Altman, "Baboon-Cell Transplant Failed, but AIDS Patient Is Improved," *The New York Times*, December 16, 1996, p. A12.

19. Gina Kolata, "Newly Found Suppressors of H.I.V. Can Be Culprits in Other Diseases," *The New York Times*, December 26, 1995, p. C3.

20. Pamela Zurer, "AIDS Suppressor May Have Been Identified," *Chemical & Engineering News*, December 11, 1995, pp. 7–8.

21. J. Travis, "Body's Proteins Suppress AIDS Virus," *Science News*, December 9, 1995, p. 388.

22. J. Madeleine Nash, "An AIDS Mystery Solved," *Time*, November 20, 1995, pp. 100–101; Kathleen Fackelmann, "Staying Alive: Scientists Study People Who Outwit the AIDS Virus," *Science News*, March 18, 1995, pp. 172–174.

23. Gina Kolata, "Scientists See a Mysterious Similarity in a Pair of Deadly Plagues," *The New York Times*, May 26, 1998, pp. F1, F5.

24. Philip Cohen, "Born Lucky," *New Scientist*, July 4, 1998, p. 24; CDC, "New Laboratory Findings May Help Explain Immunity to HIV in Thai Female Prostitutes," *CDC Press Office Geneva, Press Releases*, July 2, 1998, <http://cdcnac.org/geneva98/press/th_1500b.htm> (October 9, 1998); Linda A. Johnson, "Special Cells Linked to HIV Resistance," *The Courier-News* (Bridgewater, N.J.), July 7, 1998, p. A2.

25. Ralph T. King, Jr., "FDA Allows Large-Scale Trial of AIDS Vaccine," *The Wall Street Journal*, June 3, 1998, pp. B1, B11; Nicholas Wade, "Scientists Take First Snapshots of AIDS Virus Attacking Cell," *The New York Times*, June 18, 1998, p. A33.

26. Patty Williams, "AIDS Vaccine Race Gets Serious," *Medical World News*, July 1991, p. 28.

27. Mark Schoofs, "Body & Soul: Unsung AIDS Advance," *The Body: An AIDS and HIV Information Resource*, June 23, 1998, <http://www.thebody.com/schoofs/vaccine.html> (October 9, 1998).

28. R. Lipkin, "Tiny Microspheres Release Drugs Slowly," *Science News*, April 29, 1995, p. 262.

29. King, p. B1, B11.

30. Jaap Goudsmit, *Viral Sex* (New York: Oxford University Press, 1997), pp. 215–217.

31. Jon Cohen, "Is NIH Failing an AIDS Challenge," *Science*, February 1, 1991, pp. 518–520; Phyllida Brown, "AIDS Vaccines: What Chance of a Fair Trial?" *New Scientist*, April 27, 1991, pp. 33–37; Jon Cohen, "Is Liability Slowing AIDS Vaccines?" *Science*, April 10, 1992, pp. 168–170; Jesse Green, "Who Put the Lid on gp120?" *The New York Times Magazine*, March 26, 1995, pp. 50–57, 74, 82; Maurice R. Hilleman, "Whether and When an AIDS Vaccine?" *Nature Medicine*, November 1995, pp. 1126–1129; Jon Cohen, "A Shot in the Dark," *Discover*, June 1996, pp. 66–73; Lawrence K. Altman, "AIDS Researchers Differ on Vaccine Strategies," *The New York Times*, July 10, 1996, p. C10.

32. Jon Cohen, "Weakened SIV Vaccine Still Kills," *Science*, October 3, 1997, pp. 24–25.

33. Lawrence K. Altman, "Failed Tests on Monkeys Frustrate Hopes for AIDS Vaccine," *The New York Times*, July 3, 1998, p. A15.

34. Peter Piot, "The Science of AIDS: A Tale of Two Worlds," *Science*, June 19, 1998, p. 1844–1845.

35. Gwynne Dyer, "Africans Would Benefit from Expensive AIDS Drugs," *The Courier-News* (Bridgewater, N.J.), October 19, 1996, p. A7.

36. Michael Waldholz, "AIDS Medicine Will Cost Less in Poor Nations," *The Wall Street Journal*, June 23, 1998, p. B1.

37. Gwynne Dyer, "Good News and Bad from Conference on AIDS," *The Courier-News* (Bridgewater, N.J.), July 13, 1996, p. A5.

38. "XI International Conference on AIDS," July 8–12, 1996, <www.immunet.org/immunet/home.nsf/page/homepage> (October 9, 1998).

39. David Ho, "Killing a Killer Virus," *Forbes ASAP*, December 1, 1997, <http://www.forbes.com/asap/97/1201/179.htm> (October 9, 1998).

40. Glenn Rifkin, "All Day, Every Day, a Global Forum on AIDS," *The New York Times*, July 3, 1996, p. C7.

Glossary

AIDS—Acronym for acquired immune deficiency syndrome, a serious viral disease. (Recently some sources have used the expanded name *acquired immunodeficiency syndrome* instead, to correspond to the expanded name for HIV.)

anal intercourse—Sexual activity in which the penis of one partner is inserted into the rectum of another.

antibody—Protein produced by B cells that can react chemically with a specific antigen.

antigen—Chemical (usually a protein or complex carbohydrate) that stimulates the body's immune defenses.

antisense drug—Synthetic segment of DNA or RNA that locks on to a viral gene, blocking its instructions.

attenuated virus—Weakened virus strain used in making a vaccine.

AZT—First approved anti-HIV drug; a reverse transcriptase inhibitor; also called zidovudine (brand name Retrovir).

B cells—Lymphocytes that produce antibodies against microbes and foreign substances.

CCR5—Surface protein on white blood cells, to which HIV may bind to invade the cell. It is a chemokine receptor. People with mutant CCR5 genes are relatively resistant to HIV infection.

CD4—Protein on the surface of helper T cells, to which HIV binds in invading a cell. (*CD* is an abbreviation for "cluster of differentiation.")

chemokines—Chemical messengers that attract white blood cells to a site of infection.

chronic—Pertaining to symptoms or diseases that last a long time.

CMV retinitis—Infection of the retina of the eye by cytomegalovirus (CMV, a herpesvirus) which may lead to blindness.

condom—Protective sheath worn over the penis during sexual activity.

dementia—Progressive loss of memory and other mental functions.

DNA—Deoxyribonucleic acid; a double-stranded molecule that makes up the chromosomes in a cell; the chromosomes carry genetic information in the form of genes.

ELISA—Enzyme-linked immunosorbent assay; the most common test for HIV antibodies.

envelope—Outer covering of a virus.

gay—Popular synonym for *homosexual* (usually male).

gene—Unit of genetic information that usually contains coded instructions for the formation of a protein.

genome—Complete set of genetic instructions of an organism.

gp120—HIV envelope protein that binds to the CD4 protein on the surface of helper T cells and other target cells.

HAART—*H*ighly *a*ctive *a*ntiretroviral *t*herapy, with a combination of drugs, usually including two reverse transcriptase inhibitors and one or two protease inhibitors.

helper T cell—Type of T lymphocyte that stimulates B cells to form antibodies and also interacts with macrophages, killer T cells, and other immune-system cells; also called CD4 cell.

hemophilia—Hereditary disorder in which blood does not clot normally.

herpesviruses—Family of viruses, including herpes simplex (cold sores and genital herpes); Epstein-Barr virus (EBV), which causes mononucleosis and cancers; cytomegalovirus (CMV), which causes cellular enlargement; and varicella zoster virus (VZV), which causes chickenpox and shingles.

heterosexual—Person sexually attracted to members of the opposite sex.

HIV—Acronym for human immunodeficiency virus, the cause of AIDS. Most cases are caused by HIV-1 (HIV type 1); the less virulent HIV-2 (HIV type 2) is widespread only in West Africa.

homosexual—Person sexually attracted to members of the same sex.

immune system—Complex system of cells that defend the body from invading germs and cancerous cells; includes macrophages, B cells, T cells, and others.

incubation period—Time between exposure to a germ and the appearance of symptoms of the disease it causes.

inflammation—Body's response to tissue damage or infection, including localized redness, swelling, and pain; increased leakiness of small blood vessels lets white blood cells migrate to the site.

interferon-alpha—Protein produced by virus-infected cells that makes surrounding cells resistant to viral attack.

interleukins—Cytokines (messenger chemicals) produced by cells of the immune system to interact with each other and coordinate their activities.

IV drugs—Drugs taken by injection into a vein, such as heroin.

Kaposi's sarcoma (KS)—Normally rare form of cancer, appearing as painless purplish spots on the skin; occurs as an opportunistic infection in AIDS; caused by a herpesvirus.

killer T cells—Lymphocytes that directly attack and kill cells infected by germs, cancer cells, or other nonself cells; also called CD8 cells or cytotoxic T lymphocytes.

long-term nonprogressor—Person who has been infected with HIV for at least seven to twelve years but has a normal CD4 cell count, shows no symptoms of disease, and has had no treatment for the HIV infection.

lymphadenopathy—Swollen lymph nodes.

lymph nodes—Bean-sized organs consisting mostly of densely packed lymphocytes, clustered in the armpits, groin, and various other parts of the body.

lymphocytes—White blood cells that function in the immune system; the main types are B cells and T cells.

macrophages—Large white blood cells that can move through tissues and eat damaged body cells, invading germs, and other foreign matter.

nucleotides—Building blocks of DNA and RNA; they consist of one of five kinds of nitrogen compounds, plus a sugar (deoxyribose or ribose) and a phosphate group.

opportunistic infection—Illness caused by a virus, bacterium, or parasite that produces symptoms only in people whose immune defenses are already weakened——it takes the *opportunity* provided by the weakness in the immune system.

oral sex—Sexual activity involving contact between the mouth of one partner and the genital organs of the other.

PCP (Pneumocystis carinii pneumonia)—Opportunistic lung infection caused by a protozoa-like fungus.

PCR (polymerase chain reaction) test—Highly sensitive test for the RNA or DNA of a particular organism or virus in blood or tissue.

placebo—Harmless, ineffective substance used as a standard of comparison in testing drugs.

promiscuous—Having numerous sex partners on a casual basis.

protease inhibitor—Drug that blocks the action of HIV protease, an enzyme that cuts long protein strands into functional HIV proteins.

PWA—Person *with* AIDS.

retrovirus—Virus that contains genetic information in the form of RNA, which is used as a pattern for the host cell to manufacture DNA (genes), which then directs the production of virus components.

reverse transcriptase inhibitor—Drug that blocks the action of the HIV enzyme reverse transcriptase, which directs the formation of DNA copies of viral RNA.

semen—Fluid containing sperm, released (ejaculated) from the penis during sexual activity.

seroconversion—Development of detectable antibodies to HIV as a result of infection.

SIV—*S*imian *i*mmunodeficiency *v*irus; a retrovirus found in monkeys that is closely related to HIV.

sperm—Male reproductive cells.

T cells—Lymphocytes, including helper and killer T cells, that play various roles in the immune system.

vaccine—Substance that contains antigens or killed or weakened germs and is used to stimulate the formation of protective antibodies and/or killer T cells without causing disease.

vaginal intercourse—Sexual activity in which the penis of the male partner is inserted into the vagina of the female partner.

viral load—Amount of HIV RNA or infectious virus per unit of blood plasma, or the amount HIV RNA in tissues.

virion—Complete virus particle.

virulence—Power of a germ to cause serious illness.

wasting syndrome—Severe unintentional weight loss (mainly loss of muscle tissue).

Western blot test—Test for HIV antibodies, used to confirm a positive ELISA test result.

Further Reading

Books

Brown, Joe, ed. *A Promise to Remember: The NAMES Project Book of Letters*. New York: Avon Books, 1992.

de Solla Price, Mark. *Living Positively in a World with HIV/AIDS*. New York: Avon Books, 1995.

Douglas, Paul Harding, and Laura Pinsky. *The Essential AIDS Fact Book*. Revised edition. New York: Pocket Books, 1996.

Epstein, Steven. *Impure Science: AIDS, Activism, and the Politics of Knowledge*. Berkeley: University of California Press, 1996.

Ewald, Paul W. *Evolution of Infectious Disease*. New York: Oxford University Press, 1994.

Ford, Michael Thomas. *100 Questions & Answers About AIDS: What You Need to Know Now*. New York: Beech Tree, 1993.

Frumkin, Lyn, and John Leonard. *Questions & Answers on AIDS*. Second edition. Los Angeles: PMIC, 1994.

Goudsmit, Jaap. *Viral Sex: The Nature of AIDS*. New York: Oxford University Press, 1997.

Reitman, Judith. *Bad Blood: Crisis in the American Red Cross*. New York: Kensington Books, 1996.

Sachs, Judith. *When Someone You Love Has AIDS*. New York: Dell Publishing, 1995.

Shilts, Randy. *And the Band Played On: Politics, People, and the AIDS Epidemic*. New York: St. Martin's Press, 1988.

Stine, Gerald J. *Acquired Immune Deficiency Syndrome: Biological, Medical, Social, and Legal Issues*. Third edition. Upper Saddle River, N.J.: Prentice-Hall, 1998.

White, Ryan, and Ann M. Cunningham. *Ryan White: My Own Story*. New York: Dial Books, 1991.

Articles

"AIDS Medical Glossary." *GMHC Treatment Issues*, June 1997, pp. 1–36.

"AIDS Research—1998." *Science*, June 19, 1998, pp. 1856–1894 (special section featuring 18 articles on HIV/AIDS).

"AIDS: The Unanswered Questions." *Science*, vol. 260, May 28, 1993, pp. 1253–1293 (editorial and 10 articles).

Black, Robert F., Sara Collins, and Don L. Boroughs. "The Hidden Cost of AIDS." *U.S. News & World Report*, July 27, 1992, pp. 49–59.

Brooke, James. "In Deception and Denial, an Epidemic Looms: AIDS in Latin America." *The New York Times*, January 25, 1993, pp. A1, A6.

Burns, John F. "Denial and Taboo Blinding India to the Horror of Its AIDS Scourge." *The New York Times*, September 22, 1996, pp. 1, 10.

"Defeating AIDS: What Will It Take?" *Scientific American*, July 1998, pp. 81–107 (9 articles on the global picture, HIV therapy, viral-load tests, HIV in children, prevention, vaccines, and ethical dilemmas).

Kaminski, Matthew, and Kim Palchikoff. "The Crisis to Come (Former Soviet Union)." *Newsweek*, April 14, 1997, pp. 44–46.

Kujdych, Natalia. "Treating AIDS: Update and Outlook." *Drug Topics*, March 18, 1996, pp. 60–69.

Leland, John. "The End of AIDS?" *Newsweek*, December 2, 1996, pp. 64–73.

"Man of the Year: David Ho." Special issue, *Time*, December 30, 1996, pp. 41, 52–87.

Shenon, Philip. "After Years of Denial, Asia Faces Scourge of AIDS." *The New York Times*, November 8, 1992, pp. 1, 12.

Shenon, Philip. "AIDS Epidemic, Late to Arrive, Now Explodes in Populous Asia." *The New York Times*, January 21, 1996, pp. 1, 8.

Sullivan, Andrew. "When Plagues End: Notes on the Twilight of an Epidemic." *The New York Times Magazine*, November 10, 1996, pp. 52–62, 76–77, 84.

Internet Addresses

AEGIS & the Sisters of Saint Elizabeth of Hungary. "The AIDS Daily Update." *AIDS Education Global Information System.* 1998. <http://www.aegis.com>.

AMA. *HIV/AIDS Information Center.* 1999. <http://www.ama-assn.org/special/hiv/hivhome.htm>.

AVERT. *AIDS Education and Research Trust.* n.d. <http://www.avert.org>.

Center for AIDS Prevention Studies. "Teens Teach Kids About HIV!: Healthy Oakland Teens Projects." *What We Do.* n.d. <http://www.caps.ucsf.edu/capsweb/hotindex.html>.

CTN. "Other HIV/AIDS Resources." *Other Resources.* n.d. <http://www.hivnet.ubc.ca/Other.html>.

GMHC. *Gay Men's Health Crisis.* n.d. <http://www.gmhc.org>.

Growth House, Inc. *AIDS and HIV: General Resources.* n.d. <http://www.growthhouse.org/hivlinks.html>.

The Marketing Collaborative. *In the Best Interests of the Children.* April 8, 1997. <http://media4.hypernet.com/~ITBIC/itbic.htm>.

Medical Strategies, Inc. "AIDS and HIV." *Healthtouch Online.* 1998. <http://www.healthtouch.com/level1/leaflets/117494.htm>.

The NAMES Project Foundation. *The AIDS Memorial Quilt.* 1996–1999. <http://www.aidsquilt.org>.

Planet Q. *AIDS Virtual Library.* n.d. <http://planetq.com/aidsvl/index.html>.

SatelLife. *Program for Collaboration Against AIDS and Related Epidemics.* 1996. <http://www.healthnet.org/programs/procaare.html>.

SIS. "HIV/AIDS Resources." *Specialized Information Services.* August 1998. <http://sis.nlm.nih.gov/aidswww.htm>.

Stoller, Jason. *Pediatric HIV/AIDS Links.* April 18, 1998. <http://mail.med.upenn.edu/~jstoller.pedaids.html>.

TeenAIDS-Peercorps, Inc. *TeenAIDS-PeerCorps.* 1998. <http://www.teenaids-peercorps.com>.

UNAIDS. *The Joint United Nations Programme on HIV/AIDS.* n.d. <http://www.unaids.org>.

Index